Literature in language learning: new approaches

Edited by Ana Bela Almeida,
Ulrike Bavendiek, and Rosalba Biasini

Research-publishing.net

Published by Research-publishing.net, a not-for-profit association
Contact: info@research-publishing.net

© 2020 by Editors (collective work)
© 2020 by Authors (individual work)

Literature in language learning: new approaches
Edited by Ana Bela Almeida, Ulrike Bavendiek, and Rosalba Biasini

Publication date: 2020/09/14

Typeset by Research-publishing.net
Cover illustration, free to use, Pexels: https://www.pexels.com/photo/reading-reader-kindle-female-76942/
Cover layout by © 2020 Raphaël Savina (raphael@savina.net)

ISBN13: 978-2-490057-69-6 (Ebook, PDF, colour)
ISBN13: 978-2-490057-70-2 (Ebook, EPUB, colour)
ISBN13: 978-2-490057-68-9 (Paperback - Print on demand, black and white)
Print on demand technology is a high-quality, innovative and ecological printing method; with which the book is never 'out of stock' or 'out of print'.

British Library Cataloguing-in-Publication Data.
A cataloguing record for this book is available from the British Library.

Legal deposit, France: Bibliothèque Nationale de France - Dépôt légal: septembre 2020.

Table of contents

Notes on contributors

Editors

Ana Bela Almeida is Lecturer at the University of Liverpool where she teaches Portuguese language and lusophone studies. She studied modern Portuguese language and literature (BA, Lisbon, 2000) and Portuguese and Galician literature and visual arts (MA, Vigo, 2006). She publishes on Portuguese literature and on didactics of Portuguese foreign language. Ana Bela is one of the founding members of the Litinclass research group.

Ulrike Bavendiek is Senior Lecturer in the Department of Modern Languages and Cultures at the University of Liverpool and has been teaching German language and linguistics in higher education since 1993. She graduated with a Magister Artium in German and Japanese studies (Göttingen, 1992) and holds a Ph.D. in applied linguistics (Liverpool, 2006). She is the Director of CTELL, the University's Centre for Teaching Excellence in Language Learning.

Rosalba Biasini is Lecturer in Italian at the University of Liverpool where she teaches Italian language and culture. She studied classics and humanities (BA, L'Aquila, 2004), translation studies (MA, Manchester 2005), Italian literature (DPhil/Ph.D., Oxford, 2010), and didactics of Italian foreign language (MA, Ca' Foscari, Venice, 2013). She publishes on the field of Italian literature and didactics of Italian foreign language.

Reviewers

Nicola Bermingham is Lecturer (Assistant Professor) in Hispanic studies at the Department of Modern Languages and Cultures, University of Liverpool. She is a specialist in sociolinguistics; her work focuses primarily on the contexts of Galicia (Spain) and Cape Verde. Her research interests include migration studies, minority languages, and education.

Lisa Brennan is the Teacher Development Coordinator at the English Language Centre of the University of Liverpool, where she also teaches English for academic purposes to current and prospective international students. Her work draws on linguistics and educational psychology, and she is particularly interested in the influence of identity and culture on learning and teaching.

Silvia González studied English philology at the University of Santiago de Compostela, as well as a Masters in advanced linguistics and the PGCE. In 2014, she started her career as a Spanish teacher at the University of Liverpool. She also completed a Masters in teaching Spanish as a foreign language and she has collaborated with the University of Santiago.

Jessica Iubini-Hampton's research aims to survey the level of vitality of two minority languages: Esperanto and Modenese. Before arriving at Liverpool, Jessica completed an MA in linguistics at the University of Manchester where she was awarded a Master's Bursary by the Philological Society. Outside of her studies, Jessica acts as Membership Officer and Book Reviews Editor for the International Ecolinguistics Association.

Christian Jones is Senior Lecturer in TESOL and applied linguistics at the University of Liverpool. He is co-author of Corpus Linguistics for Grammar: A guide for research (Routledge, 2015), and Successful Spoken English: Findings from Learner Corpora (Routledge, 2017). He is also editor of Practice in Second Language Learning and Literature, Spoken Language and Speaking Skills in Second Language Learning (Cambridge University Press (2018, 2019).

Veronika Koeper-Saul is Lecturer in German in the Department of Modern Languages and Cultures at the University of Liverpool, Erasmus Coordinator for German, and Modern Languages Resources Manager in the University's Language Lounge. Her interests include approaches to independent learning, intercultural exchange, and teaching culture in the foreign language classroom.

Jordi Sánchez is currently a lecturer of Spanish at the University of Liverpool where he teaches undergraduate advanced students in their first year. He is very interested in the use of technology as a means of blended learning and is currently researching this field as well as the use of flipped classrooms in higher education and the use of Google Translate for language learning purposes.

Federica Sturani has been teaching Italian language in various institutions of higher education in the UK for over 25 years. Her long standing interest in Italian language teaching lead to several publications for the Teach Yourself series, including "Italian Tutor. Grammar and Vocabulary workbook". She is currently University Teacher at Liverpool University and Associate Tutor at Edge Hill University, Ormskirk.

Stefania Tufi is Senior Lecturer in Italian studies at the University of Liverpool, UK. Her main research interests lie within sociolinguistics. Most recently she has worked on borderscapes, language and memory, and linguistic constructions of identity in transnational spaces. Her co-edited volume, Reterritorialising Linguistic Landscape: Questioning Boundaries and Opening Spaces, was published in January 2020.

Authors

Amjad Alsyouf is Assistant Professor of English literature at Al-Balqa Applied University. He is a dynamic thinker and scholar of English and literary studies. His research interest is in using literature in language learning, poetry, comparative literature, medieval literature, and English romanticism. He has authored articles about literature, English learning, and a group of poems and intellectual essays.

Anke Bohm is currently Language Tutor in German studies in the School of Arts, Languages, and Cultures at the University of Manchester. She has taught German in Spain, Switzerland, and the UK in different institutional contexts. Her interests include flipped classroom approaches to teaching grammar and second language acquisition.

Salvatore Campisi has worked as Lector in Italian at various UK universities since 2005 (Salford, Manchester, Leeds), and his interest in independent and blended language learning has underpinned his teaching practice. He was awarded a Ph.D. with a thesis on Hermann Hesse in 2011 and is currently the Senior Language Tutor in Italian at the University of Manchester.

Géraldine Crahay is Assistant Teaching Fellow in French at Durham University. After a BA and an MA in French studies and a teacher training degree at the University of Liège (Belgium), she completed a Ph.D. at Bangor University. Her research interests include gender studies, relations between literature and science, and relations between language and dance.

Cristina García Hermoso: Fellow of the Higher Education Academy and UNILANG Assessor. Senior Teaching Fellow and Senior Tutor in modern languages and linguistics at the University of Southampton. Second prize for the ELE teacher of the year 2015, for the project "Manos a la obra", (in collaboration with Carmen Martín de León). Co-author of Palabras clave para organizar textos en español (Routledge, 2019).

Geoff Hall has been Professor of English at the University of Nottingham Ningbo China since 2011. He has taught, trained teachers, and spoken at various invited professional events in Europe, Asia, and globally. Special research areas include uses of literature in language learning, including a widely cited book for Macmillan/Springer, Literature in Language Education (second edition, 2015).

Hanna Magedera-Hofhansl, born in France, and raised in Austria, did a Master's degree in French, Portuguese, and Lutheran theology at the universities of Vienna and Strasbourg. After working at the French Cultural Institute in Vienna, she came to the University of Liverpool in 2001 and is now Lecturer in German language.

Carmen Martín de León, MPhil., is Lecturer in the Department of Modern Languages and Linguistics at the University of Southampton. She has published articles, books, and chapters on philosophy and education. Her research interests include independent learning, gamification, and literature in language teaching.

Recently, she co-authored the textbook Palabras clave para organizar textos en español (Routhledge, 2019), that focuses on discourse coherence.

Cecilia Piantanida is Assistant Professor (Teaching) in Italian at the School of Modern Languages and Cultures of Durham University. She holds a doctorate in medieval and modern languages from the University of Oxford. Her research engages with transnational and intercultural approaches to the teaching and learning of modern languages, representations of origins and (un)rootedness in contemporary writing and classical reception studies.

Idoya Puig is Senior Lecturer in Spanish at Manchester Metropolitan University. She has published a number of articles on Cervantes and sixteenth century Spanish culture. She recently published *Spanish Golden Age Texts in the Twenty-First Century* and she is currently exploring ways to harness new media to teach literary classics and to bring literature back into the language class.

Ana Reimão is Lecturer in Portuguese studies at the University of Liverpool since 2005 and a founding member of TROPO UK – the Association of Teachers and Researchers of Portuguese – which encourages scholarly research and promotes good practice on aspects of learning and teaching Portuguese in order to support the professional development of teachers.

Introduction

**Ana Bela Almeida[1],
Ulrike Bavendiek[2], and Rosalba Biasini[3]**

A renewed interest in literature is gradually emerging in the foreign language curriculum as demonstrated in recent studies (e.g. Hall, 2015; Matos, 2012; Paran, 2010; Sell, 2005). The surge of research groups and new online tools on this topic, such as the Litinclass website (https://litinclass.wordpress.com/, Almeida, Puig, & Duarte, 2016) or the Literature in Language Learning and Teaching Research Network (https://lilltresearch.net/home/, Paran & Kirchhoff, 2019) testifies to the growing relevance of this pedagogical approach to the teaching and learning of foreign languages. Both recent scholarship and class practice provide evidence that reading literary texts helps students to develop their language skills, as "[l]iterature exposes students to complex themes and fresh, unexpected uses of language" (Lazar, 1993, p. 15). Moreover, "[a]t present, students who are extensive travellers demand a different approach to the cultural dimension" (Matos, 2012. p. 7); the study of literature in the language classroom provides these students with the intercultural skills that are increasingly necessary in the contemporary globalised world. As educators, we can employ the study of literature to prepare students for dealing with the complexity of a globalised world long after graduation.

But how can this approach be adopted in teaching and learning practice? What is the best way to use songs and poetry in the language classroom? How can creative writing workshops help language learners, and what are the ethical implications of bringing literature to the language class? These were just a few

---

1. University of Liverpool, Liverpool, United Kingdom; a.almeida@liverpool.ac.uk

2. University of Liverpool, Liverpool, United Kingdom; u.bavendiek@liverpool.ac.uk

3. University of Liverpool, Liverpool, United Kingdom; rosalba.biasini@liverpool.ac.uk

How to cite: Almeida. A. B., Bavendiek, U., & Biasini, R. (2020). Introduction. In A. B. Almeida, U. Bavendiek & R. Biasini (Eds), *Literature in language learning: new approaches* (pp. 1-6). Research-publishing.net. https://doi.org/10.14705/rpnet.2020.43.1089

---

of the questions addressed at the Literature in Language Learning Conference, which took place at the University of Liverpool on the 14th of June 2019, and attracted leading experts in the fields of English and Modern Foreign Languages learning and teaching through literature[4].

Two overriding themes emerged from the conference. First, the role of literature in the language classroom in a transnational world, where the majority of language students have a multilingual and multicultural background, and where their digitally mediated experiences and identities transcend the one-nation-one-language-one-culture idea of traditional language teaching. In this context, fictional literary texts can invite students to adopt different viewpoints and thus enhance intercultural awareness. The second theme, embedded and driven by the first, is the use of literary texts for creative appropriation, the way in which students can be encouraged to actively engage with, rather than consume, literary work.

In this publication, we are pleased to offer in the form of short papers a selection of the presentations delivered at the Literature in Language Learning Conference, which captures the intellectually stimulating atmosphere of the day.

Geoff Hall opened the conference, and some elements of his keynote speech are collected in the paper that we are happy to include in this volume. Hall discovers a new relevance of literature for language learning by positioning it clearly in today's globalised world. Based on the changing profiles of language students, their often multilingual and multicultural backgrounds and their digitally mediated interconnectedness, he identifies new aims for language learning to meet the challenges of the evolving societies, arguing that literature is ideally suited to meet these challenges in the classroom. Connecting with and through literary texts, students develop 'mediation' and intercultural communication skills such as creativity, critical thinking, empathy, and emotional intelligence. Using an example from an undergraduate English class in China, Hall explains

---

4. A brief account of the event can be found here: https://www.liverpool.ac.uk/centre-for-language-excellence/news/stories/title,1158700,en.html

that different perspectives, knowledge, experiences, and values are negotiated in response to a literary text.

While acknowledging the benefits of the use of literature for language learning, **Idoya Puig**, the second keynote speaker of the conference, provides an important reminder that the actual experience of literary texts in the classroom is not always entirely positive. Students and teachers often perceive literature as 'difficult', 'time-consuming', and 'lacking in relevance', and struggle with the compulsory study of literary works in their language classes. On the other hand, recent research quoted in her speech and paper clearly demonstrates the advantages of using literary texts for language learning, advantages that are reflected in the new curricula from primary to A-level education. Puig concludes that greater flexibility regarding the choice of text, as well as clear pedagogical strategies, are needed to foster a more positive attitude towards literature in the language class.

Moving into more practical spaces, a series of case studies illustrates the use of literature in classrooms today. **Cecilia Piantanida** takes the transnational approach further, using 'migrant literature' to teach intercultural skills in an Italian language class. Migrant literature offers both an inside and an outside view of the target culture, challenging the binary oppositions of foreign versus native culture, or first versus second language speaker. Through this approach, the students develop a critical awareness of cultural difference, as Piantanida demonstrates in her empirical study of a final year Italian language class, where she uses migrant literature both as a tool and a topic. By sharing the marginal relation to the target language with the migrant author, the learners are able to reflect on the notion of identity and the effects that using a second language can have on it.

Other contributions focus on the creative engagement with literary texts, which often includes elements of creative writing or rewriting. Experimenting with *cento* poetry – the composition of poetry from verses selected from existing poems – with students in a university English class, **Amjad Alsyouf** shows that the use of appealing teaching material that allows for creative expression can counteract language anxiety. The resulting poems demonstrate deep understanding and creative use of the target language.

Imagination and creativity are also at the heart of three projects that **Carmen Martín de León** and **Cristina García Hermoso** developed to engage their students with literary texts in Spanish language. Immersing themselves in fictional worlds, learners are asked to write dialogues or continue stories, activities which allow them to use the language authentically yet creatively. In a questionnaire following these activities, the students confirmed that the tasks allowed them to build empathy and to develop their imagination.

Exploiting literature for creative purposes is shown to enhance motivation and to lead to deep appreciation of the language in class. **Ana Reimão** uses micro-contos, short and concise literary texts, to foster soft transferable skills. In her paper she recounts a Portuguese class in which clear and stimulating communicative purposes are created using micro-contos. As a consequence, her students engage affectively and cognitively in the learning process.

Salvatore Campisi uses songs to develop linguistic skills and to raise students' cultural awareness in an advanced Italian class. Campisi carefully considers the advantages and disadvantages of using music for language learning and, based on his experience with a sequence of activities based on an Italian 'ballad', explains how the activity enhanced students' engagement with Italian language and culture, helping them to develop both their linguistic and cultural competency.

Writers in residence schemes are a prestigious part of many university language departments. Such residences are often the highlight of the academic year for both students and staff. Reflecting on their experience of working with students of German before, during, and after an author's residency, **Anke Bohm** and **Hanna Magedera-Hofhansl** develop guidelines to make best use of such a visit for student learning.

As highlighted also in Puig's paper, in spite of their motivational potential, literary texts are often considered to be 'difficult' due to the 'special' language used. As a consequence, the use of literary texts is not usually recommended in the beginners language classroom. However, in her paper, **Géraldine Crahay** discusses the use of simple, playful theatrical texts at French elementary level, arguing that drama is particularly suitable for such use due to its dual nature as a written and oral text. Crahay shows how a carefully designed range of short activities helps her beginner students access and 'celebrate' the text. A creative rewriting and performing of the students' plays is the culmination of the activities and evidence of students' developing linguistic skills, as well as their creativity, cooperation, and critical thinking.

With this volume and with the organisation of the Literature in Language Learning Conference, we have offered a contribution to the current debate around the use of literature in language learning, providing what we believe are effective and original ideas for both classroom practice and scholarly investigations. We hope that these reflections and proposals will inspire language learning and teaching practice as well as further research and discussions.

Acknowledgements

We would like to thank the University of Liverpool's School of Histories, Languages, and Cultures (HLC) and the Centre for Teaching Excellence in Language Learning (CTELL) for their financial support towards the organisation of the conference and the publication of this volume.

We are very grateful to the HLC Marketing, Recruitment, and Events team for their practical and logistics help; the staff at the University of Liverpool Management School for their support on the conference day; Karine Fenix from Research-publishing.net for her priceless advice and patience; and our sponsor, European Schoolbooks, for organising a perfectly fitting display on the conference day.

We would also like to thank the speakers and delegates of the Literature in Language and Learning Conference for creating a stimulating and enriching day, and all the reviewers of this volume for their insightful work.

We would finally like to express our gratitude to Professor Diana Cullel Teixidor, Head of the Department of Modern Languages and Cultures (MLC) at the time of the conference for her time and words of encouragement, and to colleagues in MLC who gave us their advice and support. A special thanks goes to the Italian language assistants of the academic year 2018-19 for their help during the preparation as well as on the day.

References

Almeida, A. B., Puig, I., & Duarte, G. (2016). *Literature in the foreign language class project*. https://litinclass.wordpress.com/

Hall, G. (2015). *Literature in language education*. Palgrave Macmillian.

Lazar, G. (1993). *Literature and language teaching: a guide for teachers and trainers*. Cambridge University Press.

Matos, A. (2012). *Literary texts and intercultural learning: exploring new directions*. Peter Lang.

Paran, A. (2010). More than language: the additional faces of testing and assessment in language learning and teaching. In A. Paran & L. Sercu (Eds), *Testing the untestable in language education* (pp. 1-14). Multilingual matters. https://doi.org/10.21832/9781847692672-002

Paran, A., & Kirchhoff, P. (2019). *Literature in language learning and teaching*. https://lilltresearch.net/home/

Sell, J. (2005). Why teach literature in the foreign language classroom? *Encuentro, Journal of Research and Innovation in the Language Classroom, 15,* 86-93.

1 Literature, challenge, and mediation in 21st century language learning

Geoff Hall[1]

Abstract

New directions in language learning and teaching are evident today. Students bring transnational, multicultural, multilingual, and digitally mediated experiences and identities into classrooms still sometimes too much modelled on outdated one-language-one-culture-one nation ideologies. Literature's value in these new circumstances is to challenge readers to independent interpretations, learning, and creativity, with refreshed understandings of what language, culture or indeed literature might be. In this paper I review some relevant recent interventions into the foreign language education field, including a reference to the Council of Europe's (2018) Companion . I then give a brief example from my own use of a literary text in China.

Keywords: literature in multilingual and multicultural language learning, intercultural communication, literary translation, mediation, literature in CEFR Companion 2018.

1.   Introduction and 21st century language learning

In the context of the call of Kramsch (2014) to recognise new multilingual and multicultural contexts for language learning, in this paper I discuss the potential of literature for intercultural communication and mediation – Common European Framework of Reference (CEFR) (Council of Europe, 2018). New curriculum documents globally ask language educators to promote wider and more complex

1. University of Nottingham Ningbo China, Ningbo, China; geoff.hall@nottingham.edu.cn; https://orcid.org/0000-0002-8311-4024

How to cite this chapter: Hall, G. (2020). Literature, challenge, and mediation in 21st century language learning. In A. B. Almeida, U. Bavendiek & R. Biasini (Eds), *Literature in language learning: new approaches* (pp. 7-13). Research-publishing.net. https://doi.org/10.14705/rpnet.2020.43.1090

aims than simple language acquisition, including criticality, intercultural communication and empathy, creativity and innovation, independence, team working, ethics and emotional intelligence, and a host of other '21st century skills' (Naji, Subramaniam, & White, 2019). Interestingly, these documents also increasingly allocate literature a role in pursuing such aims. The Council of Europe's (2018) Companion to their globally influential 2001 'Framework' document, intended to guide the design of materials and curricula for foreign language learning, now includes explicitly aesthetic and literary aims and suggests scales and descriptors (discussion in Alter & Ratheiser, 2019; another example is Ministry of Education Singapore, 2019).

A tremendous range of people now learn a major foreign language like English for a wide variety of reasons across widely varying contexts and circumstances. In all cases, nevertheless, a foreign language comes to be part of who we are and how we identify; it can indicate our aspirations or act as a sphere for imaginative exploration. Play, pleasure, and enjoyment are central to language learning, as are anxiety and stress very often (Bigelow, 2019).

Kramsch (2009, 2014) asks us to re-think the language learner as a 'multilingual subject'. Borders between languages, cultures, and nations are porous, with migration and mobility increasingly the norm for many, together with the extended and pervasive interconnectedness the Internet promotes. The languages of literature are often mixed, hybrid, and prompt user attention to the fictitious nature of supposedly pure and correct standard national languages. The recognition of diversity and variety is common to modern understandings of language as well as basic to many literary texts, and needs to be learned and negotiated by language users. Literature prototypically deals with 'margins' of place, socioeconomic situation, class, religion, gender, language, and style. Reading literature, we need "to understand what and who is at the margins and why, and to enter the imaginative world of the marginal with compassion and radical openness" (Maginess, 2019, p. 140). The language learner, according to Kramsch (2009), has both the privileges and challenges of occupying this marginal relation to the foreign language they are learning. Traditional language learning research used static metaphors of acquisition, or input and output;

recent writers see more dynamic 'appropriation' or 'participation' in new and often challenging linguistic and cultural circumstances (Kramsch, 2014).

Second language acquisition research showed the importance of focusing on precise linguistic form for language learners (Schmidt, 2010). Literary texts often prompt such attention (Peplow, 2016). More recently, emotional engagement and feelings are highlighted as important and previously neglected elements of language learning (Bigelow, 2019). The meaningful and the moving are processed more deeply through appropriate literary texts. Critiques of commercial international and national materials used to support language learning thus suggest an important role for literature. Literature deals with 'big' issues; death, love, life, and relationships. It has personal relevance (Maley & Kiss, 2018). Commercial textbooks, by contrast, blandly observe the PARSNIP acronym referred to by Gray (2010); that is, textbook editors and writers look to avoid (in this shorthand) Politics, Alcohol, Religion, Sex, Narcotics, ISMS, and Pork – in other words, all the engaging and moving stuff which literature typically concerns itself with!

From a world-wide English perspective, Matsuda (2003) asks for representations of and explicit materials and activities to address a central issue for the English language learner, that most users of English no longer hail from white middle class nuclear families in the UK or US. Saraceni (2015) argues the need for 'a new mindset' for teachers and learners of languages in the light of actual uses of English in particular around the world today, but likewise notes the sparsity of materials and training to support such change. Best-selling and prize-winning literature in recent years quickly make apparent the relevance of such texts to these demands.

2.   Mediation

Literature reading involves 'connecting' with texts, and with others through texts, a kind of intercultural communication, and mediation, now widely specified as desiderata for language education. Cook (2010) as well as Garcia and Wei (2014) have argued for increased use of translation at all stages of language learning. For such scholars, language learning should be additive rather than subtractive, comparative rather than exclusionary. Many literary texts meet this call as appropriately multilingual and multicultural. The Companion refers to a major and typical aim of language learning as preparation for mediation roles (translation and interpreting, broadly), working between languages, rather than exclusively in one language as opposed to another (Council of Europe, 2018, p. 208).

Finally, we should also note the potential for language learners of more recent ideas of creative texts and creativity as versioning, often through the Internet, typically multimodally, through adaptations, interventions, participation, spin offs and merchandising, fan websites (e.g. Harry Potter), parodies, pastiches, and the rest. Learners confront a world of continuous change and contested interpretation and response in need of mediation, which is exactly what literature offers paradigmatically too. Today's learners more than ever before need to deal with difference, diversity, and previously unexperienced varieties and variation, and to clarify their own stance in response.

Literature should not be thought of as a fixed canon of classic texts, but as creative writings and re-writings which engage the imagination and even the passions. Such writings can be more or less popular or demanding, and accessed at various levels from personal response and leisure reading, to more intellectual analysis, as suggested by the new CEFR Companion (Council of Europe, 2018, see '3 new literature scales' and descriptors, pp. 51, 65, 76, and 116).

3.　　An example: reading Pound's 'River-merchant's wife' in China

When mediating a creative translation of a creative text, a variation on CEFR's 'Mediating a text', roughly at level C2 descriptors (Council of Europe, 2018, p. 208), my students in China are undergraduates majoring in English, and English teachers on a taught Master's programme (CEFR C1). They were asked to read Ezra Pound's (1916)[2] 'River-merchant's wife: a letter' from his collection 'Cathay', which did much in its day to confirm western stereotypes of 'the exotic East' for English language readers. My mostly Chinese students explored a text simultaneously alien but strangely familiar. Billings (2019) gives a comprehensive and critical textual account of the complex genesis of this poem and the wider collection it comes from. Briefly, knowing no Chinese, Pound wrote his own free version of a classic Chinese poem based on rough notes made by an American scholar based on his earlier studies with Japanese scholars of the Chinese classics. The poem derives ultimately from the classic 8th century Tang poet now usually known as Li Bai: here if anywhere is diversity, multilingualism, multiculturalism, and the need for mediation.

My student readers often half recognised a poem they had studied respectfully and learned by heart in high school through the layers of cultural and linguistic mediation it had undergone. How to respond to this radically translated modernist English poem? A variation on a Chinese classic? Japanese hybrid (with Japan-China relations another complicating factor)? Reading and discussion of the poem inevitably prompted, engaged even, passionate exploration of the nature and ethics of creativity and innovation, and issues in translation and intercultural communication beyond the first linguistic and aesthetic experience of the poem itself. Real communication resulted from our different perspectives and the different knowledge, experience, and values, either linguistic, social, or cultural, that teacher and students brought to the reading, with mutual and cooperative learning taking place. Critical readings included resistance to foreigners appropriating half understood texts, but then also an appreciation for the creativity of using the old to make something new for new times and the new perspectives Pound's version prompted. There is no space to report in detail here, though I urge readers to consider the poem for themselves – or better still try to use it in a class – in order to explore the claims I make for its value. It is a discomforting if sometimes beautiful poem, and that was its value for us. Here was the productive discomfort, the challenge, as well as the pleasure, a literary text can bring into a classroom. Not all classes will be at this level,

---

2. https://www.poetryfoundation.org/poems/47692/the-river-merchants-wife-a-letter-56d22853677f9

though I would note that some of the most admired lines were the simplest –
"They hurt me, I grow older" (l. 25). My urging is rather to consider the kind
of rich interactions and felt experience a well-chosen literary text can promote.

4.   Conclusion

I have sought in this brief paper to suggest that new language learning
contexts give literary texts new relevance. Issues of mediation, translation, and
intercultural communication which are inherent to much literature can be of real
interest to our multilingual and multicultural students as they strive to learn a
language and to see the value of foreign language learning. Educators now seek
to promote creativity and critical thinking in students, empathy with others, and
emotional intelligence, as well as well-being and a love for lifelong learning.
The connections literary texts embody and promote can be of great value for
these wider aims as well as for more concentrated language-focused work,
where careful choices have been made by writers and performers precisely to
foster contemplation and discussion in often complex and difficult areas which
can really engage learners.

5.   Acknowledgements

I am grateful to the reviewers of the first draft of this chapter. Their insightful
comments led me to substantial revisions and more precise formulation of my
argument.

References

Alter, G., & Ratheiser, U. (2019). A new model of literary competences and the revised CEFR
descriptions. *ELT Journal*, 73(4), 377-386. https://doi.org/10.1093/elt/ccz024
Bigelow, M. (2019). Reconsidering the role of emotion in language teaching and learning.
Modern Language Journal, 103(2), 515-516. https://doi.org/10.1111/modl.12569

Billings, T. (2019). (Ed). *Cathay. A critical edition. Ezra Pound*. Fordham University Press.

Cook, G. (2010). *Translation in language teaching*. Oxford University Press.

Council of Europe. (2018). *Common European framework of reference for languages. Companion volume with new descriptors*. https://rm.coe.int/cefr-companion-volume-with-new-descriptors-2018/1680787989

Garcia, O., & Wei, L. (2014). *Translanguaging: language, bilingualism and education*. Palgrave Macmillan.

Gray, J. (2010). *The construction of English. Culture, consumerism and promotion in the ELT global coursebook*. Palgrave Macmillan.

Kramsch, C. (2009). *The multilingual subject*. Oxford University Press.

Kramsch, C. (2014). Teaching foreign languages in an era of globalization. *Modern Language Journal, 98*(1), 296-311. https://doi.org/10.1111/j.1540-4781.2014.12057.x

Maginess, T. (2019). From the margins: the role of literature. *International Journal of Educational Research, 94*, 134-142. https://doi.org/10.1016/j.ijer.2018.12.002

Maley, A., & Kiss, T. (2018). *Creativity and English language teaching*. Palgrave Macmillan.

Matsuda, A. (2003). Incorporating World Englishes in teaching English as an international language. *TESOL Quarterly, 37*(4), 719-729. https://doi.org/10.2307/3588220

Ministry of Education Singapore. (2019). *Literature in English teaching and learning syllabus: lower and upper secondary*. https://www.moe.gov.sg/docs/default-source/document/education/syllabuses/english-language-and-literature/files/2019-literature-in-english-syllabus-(lower-and-upper-secondary).pdf

Naji, H., Subramaniam, G., & White, G. (2019). *New approaches to literature for language learning*. Palgrave Macmillan.

Peplow, D. (2016). *Talk about books. A study of reading groups*. Bloomsbury.

Saraceni, M. (2015). *World Englishes. A critical analysis*. Bloomsbury.

Schmidt, R. (2010). Attention, awareness, and individual differences in language learning. *Proceedings of CLaSIC 2010, National University of Singapore*.

2 Literature in language learning in the UK context: from current A-levels to university

Idoya Puig[1]

Abstract

The aim of this paper is to look at the impact of recent reforms to the General Certificate of Secondary Education (GCSE) and Advanced Subsidiary (AS) curriculum in the UK, which included the teaching of literature in the language classroom in an attempt to make the study of languages more attractive and to better prepare students for university. The delivery of the new GCSEs and A-Levels has served to highlight new challenges, which are hampering the intended purpose of the reforms: language GCSEs and A-Levels are perceived as more difficult than other subjects and severe grading has been confirmed. Moreover, most teachers do not view the compulsory literature element positively. Conversely, academic studies confirm the value of literature in the study of languages and various initiatives demonstrate the attractiveness and effectiveness of literature in terms of increasing motivation and enhancing language skills. In this paper, we suggest some final proposals to improve this situation.

Keywords: literature, language learning, language GCSE, A-level.

1. Manchester Metropolitan University, Manchester, United Kingdom; i.puig@mmu.ac.uk; https://orcid.org/0000-0002-1590-5799

How to cite this chapter: Puig, I. (2020). Literature in language learning in the UK context: from current A-levels to university. In A. B. Almeida, U. Bavendiek & R. Biasini (Eds), *Literature in language learning: new approaches* (pp. 15-21). Research-publishing.net. https://doi.org/10.14705/rpnet.2020.43.1091

1. Introduction and current challenges in Modern Foreign Languages (MFL) teaching

One of the latest reports by the Higher Education Policy Institute (Bowler, 2020) discusses whether the study of languages in the UK has reached a crisis point. The British Academy has also produced a number of reports, while language associations are working to measure the extent of the problem and are moving forward on influencing policy in order to reverse this decline.

> "The UK is currently nowhere near to fulfilling its linguistic potential. [...] There has been a drastic and continuing decline in the numbers studying languages at secondary school and consequently at university, especially over the past two decades. There is no indication that the Government's aim for 90% of pupils in England to take a language (modern or ancient) at GCSE by 2025 will come even close to being achieved" (British Academy, 2019, p. 5).

One of the main changes introduced in the latest education reform to improve the uptake of foreign languages was to make the study of a language compulsory in primary education. Paradoxically, this requirement was introduced at the same time as the compulsory component of languages in secondary education was removed. Thus, while taking a step forward in initiating young learners in foreign languages, the need and incentive to continue into secondary school disappeared, with highly damaging consequences (Bowler, 2020).

According to the Department of Education (DfE), the purpose and reason for studying a language at Key Stages 2 and 3 was that "learning a foreign language is a liberation from insularity and provides an opening to other cultures" (DfE, 2013, n.p.). A list of abilities published included the capacity to "appreciate stories, songs, poems and rhymes in the language" (DfE, 2013, n.p.). The value of literature in the new curriculum is therefore clearly stated. However, the reality at primary school level is that, while there has been a general improvement, there is ample room for more given that language learning remains a low priority (Tinsley & Board, 2015a).

Consequently, the uptake of languages at GCSE level has not improved, and secondary education has been unable to capitalise on the introduction of the study of a language at primary level. Moreover, DfE set a specification with descriptors limited to the performance of a 'top' student, moved the 60% controlled assessment in writing and speaking to 'all at the final exam', and imposed target language instructions, thus introducing an additional demand. There is a widespread perception, therefore, that languages are difficult, and this acts as a deterrent to those considering studying a language to A-Level. It has also now been fully recognised that there is severe grading in GCSE MFL and the Office of Qualifications and Examinations Regulation in England (Ofqual) is committed to reviewing the situation (Bowden, 2019).

The British Council identifies several other reasons why students opt not to continue with the study of languages to A-Level: students need top A-Level grades for their university applications; languages are losing out in the competition with other STEM subjects perceived as being more useful; some young people are being dissuaded from studying languages because of school fears concerning the impact on performance tables, and schools struggle to make A-Level language classes financially viable (Tinsley & Board, 2015b). The A-Level Content Advisory Board (ALCAB) recommended, as guiding principles for reform, that A-Levels should be intrinsically motivating and challenging but negotiable, and it gave careful consideration to concerns that the content was excessively ambitious (ALCAB, 2014).

Regarding literature, at least one literary work must be studied as part of a greater emphasis on knowledge and understanding of the culture and society of the language studied. However, from the beginning, there were calls in the ALCAB consultation to reconsider the compulsory study of literary works to widen the appeal of the qualification. The arguments against are that literature can appear unattractive to students and adds to the reputation of languages as being difficult (Raithby & Taylor, 2019).

Some teachers have seen the requirement as a demand imposed by several of the universities involved in the A-Level consultation. For instance, some of the books proposed for study are derived from a traditional canon of texts which is seen as distant and unappealing to students (Raithby & Taylor, 2019, p. 10). ALCAB (2014) recommended extending the range of works eligible for study to include other genres such as biographies, journals, diaries, and letters, in order to offer a wider choice to students. More needs to be done in this respect, as many schools continue to rely on texts such as (for Spanish) *La casa de Bernarda Alba*, which is poetic and powerful in symbolism, but difficult for students to understand and interpret correctly. The choice of texts and the way in which they are taught are key to the successful implementation of the literature element.

To complete this necessarily brief survey of the current situation, universities are also facing challenges given the lower numbers of students applying for language degrees and the subsequent pressure to meet target numbers. As literature, especially in a foreign language, is viewed as challenging, time-consuming, and, again, lacking in relevance today, students are less accustomed to reading, and this impacts on the use/teaching of literature in university degree programmes. All the above results in a decline in specialist literature modules at university and a shift towards more film-based modules (Davis, 2018). This, in turn, leads to the pressing need to defend the teaching of literature in the language class and to find ways to present texts in creative and attractive forms that engage students and foster the study of languages (Puig & McLaughlin, 2019).

2.　　The value of literature in the language classroom

In contrast with the situation just described, the benefits of the use of literature in the language class continue to be highlighted in recent research. Literature presents language in context: "language use in literature, then, is uniquely representative of the wider language" and it offers an opportunity to explore real human experiences and challenges (Hall, 2016, p. 458). One issue discussed is whether specific teacher training is required to use literature in the language class. Literature can be viewed as a tool just like any other used in language teaching. The focus in the language class need not necessarily be on presenting the full historical knowledge or literary background in order to study a specific canonical work, but rather using the text as a resource to enhance language teaching: "the literary text is a resource to learn from rather than an icon to be taught" (Hall, 2016, p. 464). Teachers can therefore apply the pedagogical principles they are already familiar with to prepare tasks involving the use of literary texts.

Given the growing interest in intercultural communication, literature can provide meaningful insights into the culture of a specific country and can afford an opportunity for students to develop their imagination, think for themselves, and arrive at critical conclusions. Literature is interactive and can take account of social context and student profiles, so students react and produce new meaning while also harnessing the tools provided by new technologies to communicate and share. In this case, the teacher becomes more of a facilitator who transmits enthusiasm rather than imparts information (Reyes-Torres, 2018). Recent materials published include the collection by Diamantidaki (2019) which provides a range of examples using literature in different educational contexts in order to inspire staff and students.

It is important to recognise major and small achievements in the use of literature for language learning to foster a change in mentality. English as a foreign language is taught worldwide and includes the use of literature. The British Council has produced valuable materials for the study of Shakespeare, for example, and these are widely distributed[2]. More sharing of good practice is required to enable other languages to produce similar materials and reach larger audiences.

Literary anniversaries offer opportunities to test new and creative initiatives to engage the general public with literature. One such case was the commemoration of the 400th anniversary of the death of Shakespeare and Cervantes in April 2016, when hundreds of events were organised all over the world. By way of

---

2. See for instance www.britishcouncil.cn/en/shakespearelives/learning

example, at Manchester Metropolitan University, an event was created where students from different subjects and departments came together: language students read scenes in Spanish from *Don Quijote*. They were coached by the School of Theatre staff and practised with students from the degree, who in turn performed key scenes from Shakespeare's plays and acted out a fictitious encounter between Shakespeare and Cervantes. The experience was mutually enriching and certainly generated interest in both groups of students, who took to reading books by both authors.

3.   Conclusion

The way forward must be a combination of actions implemented at different levels (Herrero, 2019): it is important to continue to have a growing, research-led discipline to support future strategies for languages, which include literature as an asset in language learning.

Curriculum content must speak to a variety of social experiences and it is vital that the pitfalls identified in the new GCSEs and A-Levels are rectified, among them severe grading and ensuring appropriate attainment levels. More flexibility should be allowed to enable new texts and media to be incorporated into the teaching of the literature component together with more teacher training opportunities.

Finally, it is necessary to continue working towards a national strategy that supports language education, makes the study of languages compulsory, and helps communicate the value of languages and literature to the wider public.

References

ALCAB. (2014). *Report of the ALCAB panel for modern foreign and classical languages.* A-Level Content Advisory Board. https://alevelcontent.files.wordpress.com/2014/07/ alcab-report-of-panel-on-modern-foreign-and-classical-languages-july-2014.pdf

Bowden, A. (2019, May 11). Modern language teaching 'under threat from tough exams'. *The Guardian*. Retrieved from https://www.theguardian.com/education/2019/may/11/modern-language-teaching-under-threat-from-tough-exams

Bowler, M. (2020). *A languages crisis?* Higher Education Policy Institute, Report 123. https://www.hepi.ac.uk/2020/01/09/action-needed-to-avert-the-growing-crisis-in-language-learning

British Academy. (2019). *Languages in the UK, a call for action*. https://www.thebritishacademy.ac.uk/publications/languages-uk-academies-statement

Davis, S. (2018). The state of the discipline. Hispanic literature and film in UK Spanish degrees. *Journal of Romance Studies, 18*(1), 25-44. https://doi.org/10.3828/jrs.2018.2

DfE. (2013). *National curriculum in England: languages programmes of study*. https://www.gov.uk/government/publications/national-curriculum-in-england-languages-progammes-of-study/national-curriculum-in-england-languages-progammes-of-study

Diamantidaki, F. (2019). *Teaching literature in modern foreign languages*. Bloomsbury Academic.

Hall, G. (2016). Using literature in ELT. In G. Hall (Ed.), *The Routledge handbook of English language teaching* (pp. 456-469). Routledge. https://www.routledgehandbooks.com/doi/10.4324/9781315676203.ch32

Herrero, C. (2019). From new literacies to transmedia literacies: the New Approaches to Transmedia and Languages Pedagogy project. In N. Becerra, R. Biasini, H. Magedera-Hofhansl & A. Reimão (Eds), *Innovative language teaching and learning at university: a look at new trends* (pp. 19-26). Research-publishing.net. https://doi.org/10.14705/rpnet.2019.32.898

Puig, I., & McLaughlin, K. (2019). *Spanish golden age texts in the twenty first century: teaching the old through the new*. Peter Lang. https://doi.org/10.3726/b14605

Raithby, K., & Taylor, A. (2019). *Teaching literature in the A level modern languages classroom*. Routledge.

Reyes-Torres, A. (2018). Literature. In J. Muñoz-Basols, E. Gironzetti & M. Lacorte (Eds), *The Routledge handbook of Spanish language teaching* (pp. 628-640). Routledge. https://doi.org/10.4324/9781315646169

Tinsley, T., & Board, K. (2015a). *Compulsory languages in primary schools: does it work?* British Council. https://www.britishcouncil.org/voices-magazine/compulsory-languages-primary-schools-does-it-work

Tinsley, T., & Board, K. (2015b). Why aren't England's A-level students learning languages? British Council. https://www.britishcouncil.org/voices-magazine/why-arent-englands-level-students-learning-languages

Transnational perspectives in the Italian language class: the uses of non-native literature to develop intercultural competence

Cecilia Piantanida[1]

Abstract

This paper explores how a transnational approach to university language classes may help develop students' intercultural competence. Researchers have shown that the integration of literature in the language class has the potential to raise intercultural competence (Deardorff, 2006), especially when migrant and travel literatures are used (Matos, 2012, Paran, 2008). I present an empirical case study of the use of migrant literature in Italian in a Learning Unit (LU) for final-year undergraduate students of Italian language – Common European Framework of Reference for languages (CEFR) C1/C2 (Council of Europe, 2001). After describing the context of the LU, I explain the rationale behind its design, outline its contents, and observe that the LU helps students to improve all canonical linguistic skills as well as intercultural abilities.

Keywords: Italian, literature, migrant writing, intercultural competence, language.

1.   Introduction

Recent debates on the future of Modern Languages (ML) in the UK have called for new transnational approaches to the discipline in order to respond

1. Durham University, Durham, United Kingdom; cecilia.piantanida@durham.ac.uk; https://orcid.org/0000-0002-6068-346X

How to cite this chapter: Piantanida, C. (2020). Transnational perspectives in the Italian language class: the uses of non-native literature to develop intercultural competence. In A. B. Almeida, U. Bavendiek & R. Biasini (Eds), *Literature in language learning: new approaches* (pp. 23-31). Research-publishing.net. https://doi.org/10.14705/rpnet.2020.43.1092

to the challenges presented by a globalised world, characterised by mobility, migration, and increasingly multilingual societies (Burdett, 2018). The Arts and Humanities Research Council (AHRC) claims that "the need for understanding and communication within, between and across diverse cultures is stronger than ever" (AHRC, n.d.). It is envisaged that university education would provide students with the skills necessary to live and work in these evolving societies, including intercultural competence.

In this context, the teaching and learning of ML according to traditional divisions into national language areas are being questioned. As Kramsch (1998) notes, the notion of language as a stable, indexical reality of national cultures should be problematised, since, in a heterogeneous social world, the relationship between language and culture is co-constructed through dialogic encounters (pp. 72-77). A transnational paradigm accounting for the impact of migration on language and culture should consider "the worldwide network of the target language" (Risager, 2006, cited in Matos, 2012, p. 116).

This paper provides an example of how intercultural learning may be embedded in the Italian language class by using a transnational approach to teaching and learning. I focus on a final-year LU on 'Literature and Interculturality', employing non-native migrant literature in Italian as both a topic and a tool to develop intercultural competence. After describing the context, I explain the rationale behind the LU's design, then outline its structure and content, and conclude with some observations on the outcomes. This paper argues that the use of non-native migrant literature in the language class may facilitate the improvement of both traditional language skills and intercultural competence, if appropriate scaffolding is employed.

I follow Deardorff's (2006) definition of 'intercultural competence' (see Figure 1 for a model). According to Deardorff (2006), "the attitudes of openness, respect (valuing all cultures), and curiosity and discovery (tolerating ambiguity) [… are] fundamental to intercultural competence", with the potential for affecting both internal and external outcomes (p. 255). Intercultural competence occurs as a "continual process of improvement" (Deardorff, 2006, p. 257) going from knowledge and comprehension of one's own culture and culturally specific socialisation and limitations (internal outcome), to a shift in one's own frame of reference, changing the way an individual interacts (external outcome), thus achieving effective communication and behaviour in an intercultural situation. When intercultural competence is most developed, an individual shows empathy, respect, and values other cultures. All elements are mutually informing each other, but can be present in the absence of others.

Figure 1. Process model of intercultural competence (Deardorff, 2006)[2], originally from Deardorff (2004)

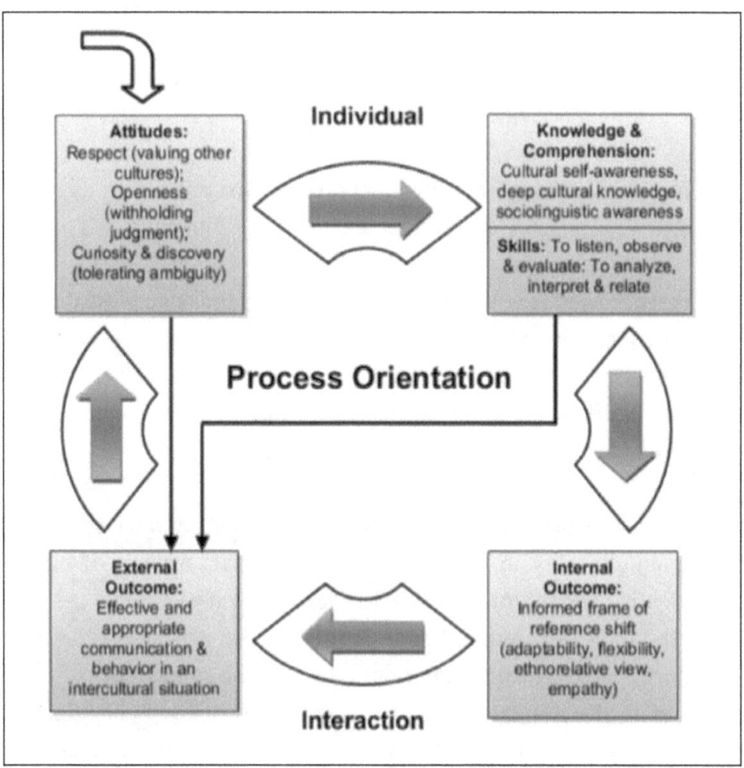

2. Reprinted by Permission of SAGE Publications, Inc.

2.   Context

The LU has been devised to fit within the context in which Italian is taught at Durham University (DU). DU's teaching and learning strategy is based on a research-led approach[3]. In the final year, after returning from a period of study or work in Italy in Year 3, students are taught in a single cohort. Students attend two weekly seminars and are expected to reach level C1/C2. All skills are practised in every seminar, although with a varied emphasis: the first seminar focuses on writing and reading comprehension skills, the second on oral skills.

Several themes are chosen to enhance students' knowledge of Italian language and culture from a transnational perspective, e.g. cultural heritage, multilingualism, history, politics, life in and outside Italy, as well as migration and cultural identities. Learning activities comprise:

- **in-class learning activities** supported by materials such as newspaper articles, academic and literary texts, TV and film clips, and music;

- **research-led learning activities** e.g. group projects, presentations, and research tasks; and

- **independent learning** supported by extra material uploaded on the virtual learning environment (Blackboard).

The LU on 'Literature and Interculturality' is the third of a tripartite teaching unit on interculturality in which students investigate aspects of nationality, cultural identity, and migration. Each LU spans over a week. In LU 1, students focus on the topics of tradition and identity. In the writing/reading seminar, they produce an analytical summary of a text on the concept of cultural roots and its uses in the Italian public discourse vis-à-vis waves of migration. In the oral seminar, students discuss tradition and its relationship to cultural and national identities. LU 2 is on the topic of immigration in Italy. Students carry

---

3. Cf. DU's website: https://www.dur.ac.uk/study/ug/learning/

out writing and translation exercises on this topic, in preparation for a final debate. LU 1 and 2 cover topics, vocabulary, and linguistic structures that provide scaffolding for approaching the final LU[4].

3.   Design

The design of the LU on 'Literature and Interculturality' takes into consideration recent scholarship on the potential of literature as a teaching tool in ML. Research shows that the integration of literature – fiction, poems, and creative writing – in the language class may raise intercultural competence, especially with non-native and travel literatures (Matos, 2012; Paran, 2008)[5]. Literary texts stimulate students' intellectual and emotional participation (Kim, 2004 cited in Hall, 2015, p. 218; Paran, 2008), encourage exploratory transformative talk (Boyd & Maloof, 2000, cited in Hall, 2015, p. 218; Paran, 2008), and boost the development of self-awareness and knowledge of the world by immersing the reader into a different context. Literature's ability to stimulate self-awareness through comparisons with 'the other' and to question established notions of identity may therefore be instrumental for the improvement of intercultural skills in the classroom.

In this context, non-native migrant and diasporic writings, which often reflect on otherness, displacement and intercultural experiences, are particularly apt teaching tools. On the one hand, they stretch the boundaries of what constitutes 'national' writing. On the other, they allow for a combined teaching approach to the theme of interculturality: teaching *with* non-native literature as a tool for improving linguistic and intercultural competence, and teaching *on* non-native literature as content, providing an opportunity to discuss the meanings of intercultural expression and interculturality itself.

For the purpose of the LU, I selected an excerpt of a literary text in Italian by Algerian writer Tahar Lamri, entitled *Il pellegrinaggio della voce* (The Voice's

---

4. On the need for scaffolding to teach languages with literary texts see Paran (2008, p. 475).

5. On definitions of literature and literary language, Hall (2015, pp. 1-46).

Pilgrimage), the author's autobiographical account of living and writing in a non-native language after migrating to Italy (see supplementary materials, Appendix 1). The learning objectives were to:

- reinforce and expand the vocabulary related to cultural identity and migration, building on previous knowledge;

- develop an appreciation of the use of figurative language in literary texts in Italian; and

- develop aspects of cultural understanding and cultural self-awareness in relation to the migrant condition, encouraging cultural empathy.

4.   The LU

The LU on 'Literature and Interculturality' is divided in a writing/reading seminar and an oral seminar. For the first seminar, preparatory work includes: finding information on migrant literature in Italian and writing a definition; watching a video-interview with Italian-Ethiopian writer Gabriella Ghermandi and taking notes[6]; and reading Tahar Lamri's text and completing comprehension and writing exercises (see supplementary materials, Appendix 1). In-class seminar activities start with a brief discussion of migrant literature and of the interview with Ghermandi. Work on the literary text follows: first, a workshop-style session inviting students to 'reread' the text and discuss their interpretations in class. As Matos (2012) argues, the process of guided re-reading is fundamental in enabling students' "intercultural reading" (pp.133-134). Secondly, in pairs, students analyse and interpret figures of speech present in the text, with attention to the use of metaphors. The session concludes with a series of open-ended questions to elicit initial responses from students, based on comparisons with their personal experiences of living abroad and using a non-native language. This is aimed at encouraging self-reflection on the topic.

---

6. See the interview here: https://www.youtube.com/watch?v=vlZmEEKEDa0

For the oral class, students are invited to take the discussion initiated in the first seminar further by working on creative group projects reacting to Lamri's text and the topic of interculturality. Creative responses are encouraged (see supplementary materials, Appendix 2). Research suggests that multicultural exposure can enhance creativity, "allowing one to see new perspectives on familiar things" (Bee Tin, 2013, p. 388). At the same time, by stimulating the construction of new meaning, creative activities help learners stretch their language (Bee Tin, 2013, p. 387). In the seminar, students showcase their group projects in ten minute presentations, followed by questions from peers. In the academic year 2018/2019 and 2019/2020, projects included a student-produced video on Italian communities in Durham, in-class dramatisations of a talk-show on migration and the migrant condition, TV news on the migrant crisis in Italy, and students' experiences in their year abroad.

5.   Observations

My own observations in class and module evaluations revealed an overall positive student response to the LU on 'Literature and Interculturality'.

Coursework and assessment showed that students fulfilled the LU learning objectives (see supplementary materials, Appendix 3): the majority were able to write about migration and interculturality in Italy, some in relation to their own condition, and to recognise and contextualise metaphorical language. Class observation suggests that students developed critical awareness of cultural difference and of one's own culturally specific socialisation. The autobiographical aspect of Lamri's text was particularly impactful, kindling discussion on the migrant condition, rootlessness, and the effects of operating in a non-native language on one's own personal identity. Conversations reacting to the text often employed cross-cultural comparisons between students' own experiences and Lamri's account, as well as discourses valuing migration, multilingualism, and multiculturality. These developments coexisted with world-views sometimes firmly anchored on 'national paradigms' and on binary oppositions between 'culture of origin' versus 'foreign culture', or 'native' versus 'migrant'.

In module evaluations, the group-project presentation was often singled out as the favourite element of the whole module. In class, students showed interest in the topic and all learning activities chosen. As often when literature is employed in L2 classes, most student discussions focused on comprehension, fewer on interpretation and evaluation (Kim, 2004, cited in Hall, 2015, p. 219). Oral reports from students evidenced that the analytical work on the literary text was sometimes perceived as difficult. This suggests that, depending on the cohort's abilities, further scaffolding and contextualisation may be needed to use literature in the language class.

6. Conclusions

This paper has described a LU that employs a transnational approach to the teaching of Italian, addressing the AHRC's (n.d.) call for a novel teaching environment that fosters intercultural exchange. As this paper has argued, non-native migrant literature may successfully be employed in university Italian classes to develop both linguistic and intercultural competences, if appropriate scaffolding is provided. While developing all canonical linguistic skills, students also cultivated transferable skills such as cultural understanding and cultural self-awareness, as well as project management and creative skills.

7. Supplementary materials

https://research-publishing.box.com/s/ncsoxcgi2mn44sssbnbnhlry0iqlxucp

References

AHRC. (n.d.). Translating cultures. *Arts and Humanities Research Council.* https://ahrc.ukri. org/research/fundedthemesandprogrammes/themes/translatingcultures/

Bee Tin, T. (2013). Towards creativity in ELT: the need to say something new. *ELT Journal, 67*(4), 385-396. https://doi.org/10.1093/elt/cct022

Boyd, M., & Maloof, V. M. (2000). How teachers build upon student-proposed intertextual links to facilitate student talk in the ESL classroom. In J. K. Hall & L. S. Verplaetse (Eds), *Second and foreign language learning through classroom interaction* (pp.163-181). Erlbaum.

Burdett, C. (2018). Moving from a national to a transnational curriculum: the case of Italian studies. *Languages, Society & Policy.* http://www.meits.org/policy-papers/paper/moving-from-a-national-to-a-transnational-curriculum-the-case-of-italian-st

Council of Europe. (2001). *Common European framework of reference for languages: learning, teaching, assessment. Structured overview of All CEFR Scale.* https://rm.coe.int/168045b15e

Deardorff, D. K. (2004). *The identification and assessment of intercultural competence as a student outcome of international education at institutions of higher education in the United States.* Unpublished dissertation. North Carolina State University, Raleigh.

Deardorff, D. K. (2006). Identification and assessment of intercultural competence as a student outcome of internationalization. *Journal of Studies in International Education, 10*(3), 241-266. https://doi.org/10.1177/1028315306287002

Hall, G. (2015). *Literature in language education* (2nd ed.). Palgrave Mcmillan.

Kim, M. (2004). Literature discussions in adult L2 learning. *Language Education, 18*(2), 145-166.

Kramsch, C. (1998). *Language and culture.* Oxford University Press.

Matos, G. A. (2012). *Literary texts and intercultural learning: exploring new directions.* Peter Lang.

Paran, A. (2008). The role of literature in instructed foreign language learning and teaching: an evidence-based survey. *Language Teaching, 41*(4), 465-496. https://doi.org/10.1017/s026144480800520x

Risager, K. (2006). *Language and culture: global flows and local complexity.* Multilingual Matters.

4 Cento as a creative writing approach to language learning

Amjad Alsyouf[1]

Abstract

Creative writing can be both an effective and attractive English learning activity at university departments where students speak English as a Second Language (ESL). Language skill courses might not be always effective enough in improving learners' communicative skills and motivating them to learn, particularly when adopting old style grammar-translation based methods. Involving creative writing as a method to teach language can play a significant role in prompting the students to improve their communicative skills. This study proposes employing a creative writing course as a new method to address L2 learners lacking motivation. It particularly relies on using cento poetry as a teaching activity. A cento is a poem made up of lines the learner selects from different poems by one or more poets. The learner consequently has to read several poems, understand their linguistic structures, and grasp the meaning of their vocabulary to begin writing their own work. It is against this background that this study examines the advantages of using cento poetry in ESL classes aiming to enhance language learning.

Keywords: cento, creative writing, language learning, ESL, L2.

1. Al-Balqa Applied University, Salt, Jordan; amjad.alsyouf@bau.edu.jo; https://orcid.org/0000-0001-8490-0433

How to cite this chapter: Alsyouf, A. (2020). Cento as a creative writing approach to language learning. In A. B. Almeida, U. Bavendiek & R. Biasini (Eds), *Literature in language learning: new approaches* (pp. 33-39). Research-publishing.net. https://doi.org/10.14705/rpnet.2020.43.1093

1. Introduction

Learners of English as L2 have often pragmatic reasons for learning the language that constitute an essential intrinsic motivation for the process. Undergraduate students who study English as a major or in a foundation course, however, might not have the intrinsic motivation to learn English as an effective communicative language; their concern would mostly rest in matters of passing exams and fulfilling programme requirements. Hadfield and Dörnyei (2013) argue that the concern with passing exams is an extrinsic motivating factor associated with the 'ought-to L2 self' that concentrates on future goals rather than L2 effective acquisition. Departments of English at universities should be aware of this problem, and need to adopt new creative methods that can assist the traditional approaches to teach English in the classroom. Involving creative writing as a method to learn and teach languages in this regard can play a significant role in stimulating students to improve their communicative skills, as it encourages cooperative learning where the students begin to personally contribute to the classroom teaching/learning activities. Cento can then be employed as an effective creative writing tool to assist L2 teaching in this context as it mostly relies on the work of the students. A cento is a poem made up of lines the learner selects from different poems by one or more poets; thus it engages the learner in a language activity that can make L2 acquisition efficient and enticing.

2. Rationale

Jiménez (2015) points out that students' lack of motivation forms one of the main factors that affect language acquisition of ESL learners, and that "demotivated" students prefer to "abstain from participating" in class activities and require a facilitation of "their participation in order to keep them motivated to learn" (p. 225). The attractiveness of reading and writing poetry can hence play a significant role in motivating L2 students to interact and learn. Koçak (2010) argues that learners' limited opportunities of practice and communication results in creating anxiety that negatively affects the process of learning (p. 141). A cento class can deal with this as it gives the opportunity to everyone in the classroom to practise and participate since each learner has to create their own written work and then communicate it to others as demonstrated below.

Brown (2007) and Ellis (2008) analyse different factors related to language learning and successful language acquisition. They focus on the classroom environment and its contribution to create effective instruction and engage L2 learners in practising the spoken language they learn. Teaching cento can serve this purpose as it can involve attractive teaching materials like colourful poetry books, poetry posters, poetry including images on the smart-board, online poetry, and recordings of auditory recitations. These materials definitely help in creating an exciting classroom environment and improving language learning.

Part of the problem faced by L2 learners is lexical insufficiency. Rich acquisition of L2 vocabulary is necessary for developing language fluency. Poetry in this respect can function as a prolific source of vocabulary for the language of poetry appeals to the mind where it is easily memorised and from which it is smoothly retrieved (Alsyouf, 2019, p. 65). Munden (2015) similarly argues that poetry engages the teachers and their students "by the fundamental connection between poetry and the memory" (p. 68). Employing poetry in the L2 classroom is therefore a useful language learning tool as it introduces the learner to a rich world of idioms. In a study that examines the benefits of using poetry in language learning, Alsyouf (2019) states that many poems rely on an intensive use of imaginative language that renders the learning process enjoyable. The teacher should therefore select joyful poetry as far as learning idioms and spirit lifting is the purpose of the L2 class.

3.   Discussion

3.1.   Using cento as an L2 learning activity

A cento is a work composed by a random number of verses purposefully selected from a group of poems, and arranged together in an order that creates a new meaningful poem. Applying this activity in L2 learning classes imposes a sequence of steps that includes reading several works of poetry, selecting particular favourite lines from them, developing a clear understanding of their language, and then beginning to write a new poem out of the selected lines. Implementation of a cento activity in L2 learning classrooms is simple but effective at the same time. Kamata (2019) highlights the advantages of employing cento composition in English as a Foreign Language (EFL) classrooms, arguing that cento is easy to compose as it helps learners to "come up with original ideas on the spot" (p. 6). It offers an opportunity to examine the selected text and understand its meaning before learners start their own composition. Creating a cento in this context becomes an effortless but efficient approach to L2 learning.

3.2. Application

Cento for L2 learning was applied by the researcher in an ESL classroom. Learners were given selections from Shakespeare's sonnets and assigned to compose a cento ranging from five or six lines out of different ones of them. They were directed to adopt a theme prior to composition, thus the created poem should meet the chosen theme. They were requested also to count the number of the new words/phrases they learned from practising cento creation, and were informed that all types of dictionaries were available to use. They finally had to read aloud the cento they wrote. The results are shown in selected samples below created by learners with previous poetry interests (Table 1, Table 2, Table 3, and Table 4).

Table 1. Learner 1

Verse	Sonnet #	Line #
For precious friends hid in death's dateless night,	XXX	6
And with old woes new wail my dear time's waste:	XXX	4
When lofty trees I see barren of leaves,	XII	5
Nor gates of steel so strong but Time decays.	LXV	8
Now with the drops of this most balmy time,	CVII	9
No longer mourn for me when I am dead.	LXXI	1

Theme: Death closes everything, including nostalgia and all bad feelings of loss.

Table 2.   Learner 2

Verse	Sonnet #	Line #
Now is the time that face should form another;	III	2
And see the brave day sunk in hideous night;	XII	2
I sigh the lack of many a thing I sought,	XXX	3
Then can no horse with my desire keep pace.	LI	9
To shun the heaven that leads men to this hell.	CXXIX	14

Theme: Facing reality with new ways and thoughts.

Table 3.   Learner 3

Verse	Sonnet #	Line #
When I behold the violet past prime,	XII	3
Calls back the lovely April of her prime;	III	10
Kissing with golden face the meadows green,	XXXIII	3
Even in the eyes of all posterity	LV	11
The hand that writ it, for I love you so,	LXXI	6
That in black ink my love may still shine bright.	LXV	14

Theme: True love eternally lives to be noticed even by coming generations.

Table 4.   Learner 4

Verse	Sonnet #	Line #
O, no! it is an ever-fixed mark,	CXVI	5
Despite of wrinkles, this thy golden time.	III	12
When I do count the clock that tells the time,	XII	1
All losses are restor'd and sorrows end.	XXX	14
That in black ink my love may still shine bright.	LXV	14

Theme: Love grows up and survives despite sorrows.

Establishing harmony between the predetermined theme and the selected poetry lines created a challenge for the learners because they needed to keep an eye on the meaning each used line contributes to the whole construction. Every word, phrase, and sentence in a selected line was consequently thoroughly investigated by the learner. The outcome of this practice is invaluable in terms of L2 learning since using cento employs an amalgam of reading comprehension and writing composition activities practised simultaneously by the learner.

After the cento activity, the researcher provided the sample group with a questionnaire that included five points regarding vocabulary, composition, element of enjoyment, dictionary usage, and a free space to mention any other ESL merits of the cento class; students gave the following feedback. First, the activity is useful for vocabulary acquisition as it provides the learners with new idioms ranging between two to six words/phrases for each learner included in the practice. Secondly, it helps learners to get familiar with sentence structures as they have to keep their cento cohesive and coherent and so they begin to think about language as discourse. These two points conform to the British Council's (n.d.) perspective that literature offers "a rich source of linguistic input" and helps learners by "exemplifying grammatical structures and presenting new vocabulary" (n.p.). Students also added that creating a cento renders the learning process interesting and enjoyable, and pointed out that it strengthens the connection between the learner and the dictionary.

4.   Conclusion

Cento is evidently an exciting and useful method of L2 learning as the study demonstrated through discussion and application. The sample group indicated additional merits of the cento activity in the questionnaire. They mentioned that it gave them confidence to write a composition, introduced them to new ways of expressing feelings and thoughts, gave them the opportunity to show creative writing skills, and trained their minds on imagination and creativity. The researcher noticed that those merits contributed to the enhancement of L2 learners' intrinsic motivation. The study recommends the application of cento for L2 learning for the above benefits, and for its value as an untraditional method of instruction and inexhaustible source of language.

References

Alsyouf, A. (2019). Creative writing as an effective method of learning English as a foreign language: a case study of Arab learners. *Folio, Journal of the Materials Development Association, 19*(1), 64-68.

British Council. (n.d.). Using literature - an introduction. *TeachingEnglish.* https://www. teachingenglish.org.uk/article/using-literature-introduction

Brown, H. D. (2007). *Principles of language learning and teaching* (5th ed.). Pearson Education.

Ellis, R. (2008). *The study of second language acquisition* (2nd ed.). Oxford University Press.

Hadfield, J., & Dörnyei, Z. (2013). *Motivating learning.* Routledge.

Jiménez, G. V. (2015). Three communication difficulties of EFL students. *Revista de Lenguas Modernas, 23*(2015), 221-233. https://doi.org/10.15517/rlm.v0i23.22347

Kamata, S. (2019). *Writing cento poems in a Japanese EFL classroom.* White paper. https://www.researchgate.net/publication/330213175

Koçak, M. (2010). A novice teacher's action research on EFL learners' speaking anxiety. *Procedia – Social and Behavioral Sciences, 3,* 138-143. https://doi.org/10.1016/j.sbspro.2010.07.025

Munden, P. (2015). Poetry by heart. In G. Harper (Ed.), *Creative writing and education* (pp. 68-70). Multilingual Matters,. https://doi.org/10.21832/9781783093540-010

Exploring literary texts to develop students' creative writing skills: proposed activities for Spanish as a foreign language

Carmen Martín de León[1] and Cristina García Hermoso[2]

Abstract

Literary texts offer a rich environment for language learning that teachers can exploit to develop not only students' linguistic (pragmatic, discursive) and cultural skills, but also communication and creative skills. In our study, we have used literature with different writing activities that involved the use of students' imagination and creativity. In order to develop these skills, which require students' communicative competence as well as their imagination, we need for them to be able to create the meaningful contexts that lie within fictional stories. The assumption is that, as students become familiar with the characters in the novels, they will be able to recreate situations that make sense for those very stories, generating a shared world in which they could immerse themselves. In that shared world, they would be able to participate in possible dialogues and build stories that could have taken place, thus developing their creative and communicative skills. In this paper, we show how the literature-based learning activities that we have designed following this hypothesis have helped students empathise with characters in novels and imagine fictional worlds. Such new fictional worlds have in turn empowered students to communicate in Spanish in an authentic way, that is, in a way that is similar to that of the characters in the novels.

1. University of Southampton, Southampton, United Kingdom; cmdl1f11@soton.ac.uk; https://orcid.org/0000-0001-9642-1819

2. University of Southampton, Southampton, United Kingdom; c.garcia-hermoso@soton.ac.uk; https://orcid.org/0000-0002-6693-6958

How to cite this chapter: Martín de León, C., & García Hermoso, C. (2020). Exploring literary texts to develop students' creative writing skills: proposed activities for Spanish as a foreign language. In A. B. Almeida, U. Bavendiek & R. Biasini (Eds), *Literature in language learning: new approaches* (pp. 41-49). Research-publishing.net. https://doi.org/10.14705/rpnet.2020.43.1094

Keywords: literature, creativity, writing skills, linguistic competence, language teaching, foreign language.

1. Introduction

Literary texts are considered to be 'controlled inputs', capable of offering an appropriate level for the learner (Jouini, 2008). Much like newspapers and magazines, literary texts are authentic documents, for although they have not been designed for language teaching purposes, they allow an interactive process of communication between authors, students, and teachers as mediators. However, fictional works of literature tend to go beyond newspapers and magazines when it comes to combining oral and written language. This combination of discourses makes literature an ideal resource from which students can envisage and create situations in which they can act authentically (Sanz Pastor, 2006). That is to say, on the one hand, when recreating situations, students will be manoeuvring in a communicative environment in which they will be able to share ideas, emotions, and information. On the other hand, by acting authentically, their verbal communication process for problem solving, negotiation of meanings and exchange of reactions will respond to a specific objective and will follow normal communication mechanisms (Fernández, 2001). Additionally, the relative length of novels gives students the necessary time to become familiar with the stories, characters, and plot development of the text, which will be required for the development of the students' creative skills.

2. Use of literature in language learning: developing stories

In order to exploit literature for creative purposes, we have been exploring how best to assist students to build fictional contexts and recreate situations. Fictional reality in literature depends largely on the imagination of the reader since, as Ritlyová (2014) states, even just reading a text without additional tasks can be considered creative because, by doing so, readers develop their fantasy. However, not all students have the same degree of imagination, but encouraging students' empathy towards the characters is an effective way to open and nurture their imagination. Students get into the characters' shoes and live through their adventures; by doing this, they become creative and construct meaningful and conceivable contexts (Martín de León & García Hermoso, 2016). These contexts created by the students will help them predict possible reactions of fictional characters to a given narrative, encouraging students not only to build and improve reading skills (Jouini, 2008) but also to develop creative writing skills.

3.   Activities

The following three cases illustrate three projects relating to our teaching practice. In each case, students identify with characters and predict their possible behaviours (Table 1).

Table 1.   Three cases

	Targeted students	**Materials**	**Methodology**	**Creative Task**
Case 1	Higher education students of Spanish as a second language (CEFR B2/C1)	Extracts from Don Quixote and El Mundo de Custodio I	Parallel texts methodology	Writing dialogues
Case 2	Primary school students (in Spain), language and literature (1° ESO)	El Mundo de Custodio I and II	Parallel texts methodology Gamification	Completing a chapter
Case 3	Higher education students of Spanish as a second language (CEFR B2/C1)	A choice between Mario Vargas Llosa and Isabel Allende's novels	Scaffolding methodology	Interviewing a character

3.1.   Case 1

In our first project, we used the *parallel texts methodology*, consisting of working hand in hand with two literary texts whose main characters share a number of behavioural or personality traits (Martín de León & García Hermoso, 2016).

This methodology allowed students to develop strategies to build meaningful contexts needed to work with idiomatic expressions and to detect and develop sarcasm. In Case 1, students had to write potential dialogues for an extract of one of the texts given. The students completed the task successfully and the dialogues they created fitted well with the characters' language and personalities. Examples of lines produced by two different groups of students in response to the same script are available in the supplementary materials (Annex 1).

3.2.   Case 2

For our second project, we used the same methodology as in Case 1, but also included *gamification*, based on the inclusion of elements that are characteristic of games in the classroom (Foncubierta & Rodríguez, 2014). To help students recognise the characters' speech and to immerse themselves in the cultural context of the novel *El Mundo de Custodio I*, we prepared a board game that students played in class[3]. To evaluate the success of this activity, we asked them to write the ending of an incomplete chapter in the sequel *El Mundo de Custodio II*, which they had not yet read. The students were able to successfully complete the chapter, using their creativity and conveying the personalities of the main characters in their dialogues. Examples of texts produced by a group of students are available in the supplementary materials (Annex 2).

3.3.   Case 3

For this project, we applied *scaffolding methodology*, which works by guiding and supporting students to reach their potential level through learning materials that promote the progressive use of communication skills (Martín de León & García Hermoso, 2020). In this particular case, the support given to students consisted of activities carried out in the classroom: listening to radio programmes and reading newspaper articles, which included interviews with authors Isabel Allende and Mario Vargas Llosa. We also offered students the chance to carry out a fictional interview with Celestina, the main character of

---

3. http://elmundodecustodio.com/materiales-para-profesores-de-lengua-y-literatura-de-educacion-primaria-y-secundaria/

Fernando de Rojas' work first published in 1499 (Duque, Martín de León, & García Hermoso, 2019).

Whereas in Cases 1 and 2 students had to step into the novel so they could recreate scenes and dialogues, with this third project they had to bring the fictional character out of the novel and interview them in order to empathise with their emotions. Examples of texts produced by a group of students are available in the supplementary materials (Annex 3).

4.   Methods

We have carried out pedagogical research to test how empathising with characters – as in Case 3 – helped students. Students had also been asked to interview a fictional character from a novel by either Isabel Allende or Mario Vargas Llosa.

We asked all 14 students who took part in the creative writing activity to participate in our study and complete a questionnaire, which consisted of six questions intended to assess the participants' opinions regarding the usefulness of the activity they completed. Nine participants answered the questionnaire.

5.   Results and discussion

The responses to the questionnaires (Figure 1) confirm that all participants felt the interviews carried out in Case 3 had helped them understand the personality, the behaviour, and the fictional world of the characters they interviewed. In principle, participants did not believe that interviewing their characters had helped them to better understand their language. However, in answering the last question (Figure 3) they highlighted specific linguistic gains from this activity.

It is interesting to see that, when asked if they could create an alternative ending or a new chapter where they could include the information gathered from their interviews (Figure 2), most of the students preferred the option of writing a new chapter. A possible reason for this could be that this type of activity collected information that comes from the point of view of a single character in the novel. In this sense, the responses of the characters would help students dig into certain aspects of their lives.

Figure 1. Aspects of my character that I have been able to know thanks to this activity

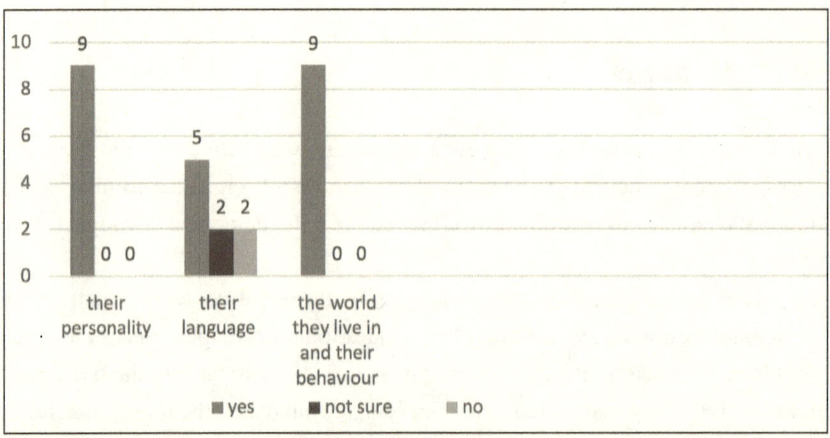

Figure 2. Creative activity that I would feel confident doing after having completed the interview

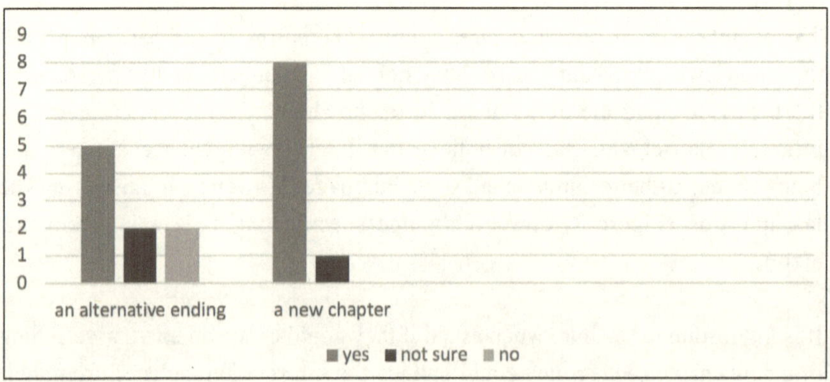

Although one of nine participants indicated they were not sure if they would feel confident creating a new chapter, none of them indicated they could not engage in this task. Additionally, we were pleased to see that more than half of our participants felt they could create an alternative ending, given that the skills required to offer a new ending go beyond what has been achieved by empathising with the character and the contextualisation. It was encouraging to see that some students felt confident they had the tools to recreate the world of the character and engage in such a task at this stage.

As far as perception of linguistic gains is concerned, eight of nine students responded that the activity had had a positive impact on their linguistic skills, especially in terms of vocabulary, style, and register (Figure 3).

Figure 3. Contribution of this activity to students' language learning

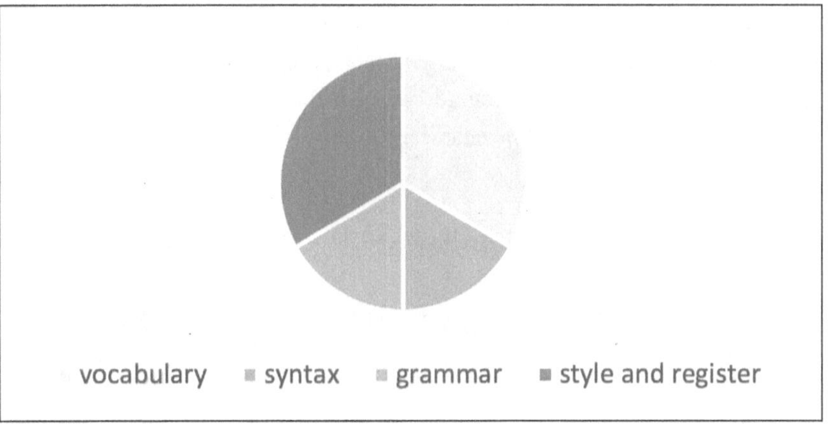

6.   Conclusion

Our goal when working with literature was to help our students empathise with novel characters and become familiar with their fictional worlds. We hypothesised that once students knew the characters, they would have the tools to act and communicate in an authentic fashion, as described in the introduction, given that they would have become familiar with the context in which to do so.

Successful completion of the creative activity in each of the three cases presented in this paper has demonstrated students' ability to recreate the world of their characters and act in an authentic way.

With Case 3, we wanted to find out to what extent the activities we had prepared for them had contributed to achieving our goal. That is, if the activities we offered our students in our teaching practice provided them a space where they could build empathy towards the characters, and contributed positively to the development of their imagination when using creative writing skills. The results we have observed clearly confirm that the activity proposed has successfully achieved our goals.

In subsequent studies, it would be interesting to work with one single character of one novel to have the opportunity to compare the interviews of different students for the same character and to account for the different perspectives in which the students perceive the character.

7.   Supplementary materials

https://research-publishing.box.com/s/16xt1fr9vv584j14kq52txhzbdgnioh4

References

Duque, E., Martín de León, C., & García Hermoso, C. (2019). *Palabras Clave para organizar textos en español*. Routledge. https://doi.org/10.4324/9780429490194

Fernández, S. (2001). (Ed.). *Tareas y proyectos en clase: español lengua extranjera*. Edinumen.

Foncubierta, J. M., & Rodríguez, C. (2014). *Didáctica de la gamificación en la clase de español*. Edinumen.

Jouini, K. (2008). *El texto literario en la clase* de E/LE: propuestas y modelos de uso. *Didáctica, Lengua y Literatura, 20,* 149-176. https://revistas.ucm.es/index.php/DIDA/article/view/DIDA0808110149A/18965

Martín de León, C., & García Hermoso, C. (2016). *"Manos a la obra" – trabajo con textos paralelos en el aula E/LE: contextualización de las unidades fraseológicas.* https://fiape.org/wp-content/uploads/2018/07/actas-iv-congreso.pdf

Martín de León, C., & García Hermoso, C. (2020). *Suitable activities for independent learning.* In A. Plutino, K. Borthwick & E. Corradini (Eds), *Innovative language teaching and learning at university: treasuring languages* (pp. 47-52). Research-publishing.net. https://doi.org/10.14705/rpnet.2020.40.1065

Ritlyová, A. (2014). Creative use of literature in language teaching. *škola tvorivosti 2, online konferencia 29* (pp. 94-102). https://www.pulib.sk/web/kniznica/elpub/dokument/Germuskova2/subor/Ritlyova.pdf

Sanz Pastor, M. (2006). *Didáctica de la literatura: el contexto en el texto y el texto en el contexto.* Universidad Antonio de Nebrija.

6 Developing soft skills with micro-fiction: a close-reading experience

Ana Reimão[1]

Abstract

Micro-contos, or micro-fiction, are very short and concise literary texts that require close-reading and inference from the reader. In this case study, I will describe how I have used these widely available texts in a Portuguese A2/B1 language module to develop analytical and other soft skills. I will demonstrate how this activity meets Tomlinson's (2011) universal principles for materials development in language teaching, namely, exposing learners to meaningful input highlighting linguistic features as well as enabling learners to engage affectively and cognitively in the learning experience. Finally, I will give details of how it has been received by students.

Keywords: soft skills, critical thinking, affectivity, transferable skills, learner-centred.

1.   Introduction and context

According to the British Academy report (Born Global, 2016), graduates with languages are highly valued by UK employers (pp. 4-5). Nevertheless, fostering the development of soft skills and other competencies alongside language proficiency has become a priority for foreign language teachers in recent years. This case study describes the activities used with a group of 14 students of Portuguese in Semester 1 of their second year. Students will have studied the language for one year only and achieved a Common European Framework of

---

1. University of Liverpool, Liverpool, United Kingdom; a.reimao@liverpool.ac.uk

How to cite this chapter: Reimão, A. (2020). Developing soft skills with micro-fiction: a close-reading experience. In A. B. Almeida, U. Bavendiek & R. Biasini (Eds), *Literature in language learning: new approaches* (pp. 51-58). Research-publishing.net. https://doi.org/10.14705/rpnet.2020.43.1095

Reference for languages (CEFR) A2 level. This module, with three weekly contact hours, relies heavily on independent study and aims to consolidate linguistic knowledge and take students onto B1 level by the end of the semester (12 weeks, 30 contact hours, and 120 hours of independent study).

2.   Theoretical framework

The issue that arose during module design was how to develop soft transferable skills while developing the target language using age and level appropriate materials in this fast-paced Portuguese language module. I initially started to work with *micro-contos* because they are very short literary texts that are self-contained. This means that, unlike when using a novel or short story, the full length of the text can be addressed and explored during the class, leaving ample time for discussion and other activities. These short texts are also widely available in many languages through online collections in blogs, webpages, and social media, such as *twitterature* or *instapoesia*, for instance.

In my experience, many language students are reluctant to read and study literary works, but research suggests that these materials aid the development of intercultural awareness, critical thinking and problem-solving alongside language proficiency (Almeida & Puig, 2017). Therefore, I wanted to encourage students to make the most of these authentic learning materials by modelling reading strategies and demonstrating that literature can be fulfilling, challenging, thought-provoking and – essentially – fun.

Further to this, I wanted to better support the transition from CEFR A2 to B1 level. Admittedly, in the first year of studies there is an emphasis on accuracy and accumulating a wide range of basic vocabulary and grammatical structures. However, this sometimes translates into a mindset where learners think that accuracy trumps content. As students prepare for a placement either working or studying in a Portuguese speaking country during their third year abroad, it is important to challenge this mindset by encouraging students to focus on communicating meaningful ideas.

In the first instance, I found guidance in materials development in Tomlinson's (2011) basic principles. This author takes into account research on L2 acquisition and proposes a set of useful parameters: learners must be exposed to rich and meaningful input; learners must be engaged cognitively and benefit from using the same mental resources they typically use in L1; learners benefit from noticing salient features and discovering how they are used; learners need opportunities to use language to achieve communicative purposes (Tomlinson, 2011, p. 7). These guidelines sum up a well-rounded learner-centred approach to language teaching, with a focus on both input and output. In addition, Tomlinson stresses the importance of positive affect and suggests a few strategies to enable it which I will later discuss.

With these considerations in mind, I created the set of language learning activities described below. They are meant to support learners to bridge the gap between CEFR levels A2 to B1, but may be useful in other levels.

3. Activity description

I conducted this activity over two one-hour lessons. The aim was to develop analytical skills that would enable learners to write a critical review in Portuguese, as part of the assessment; see full instructions in Figure 1.

Figure 1. Instructions[2]

1st Coursework Assignment

Please write a critical review in Portuguese (min. 300 words) on one or two micro-contos of your choice. The micro-conto(s) must be originally written in Portuguese and transcribed in your assignment (indicating the source) but excluded from the overall word count. Please note that you should follow these reading guidelines:

a. De que trata o micro-conto? Faça uma análise expondo as suas três camadas: tema, acontecimentos que levaram ao momento descrito no conto, descrição e análise dos personagens.
b. Imagine um final ou final alternativo para o(s) micro-conto(s).
c. Explique porque escolheu o/cada micro-conto e a sua relevância para a cultura contemporânea.
d. No caso de ter escolhido dois contos, pode refletir sobre as suas diferenças e semelhanças.

2. Translation from the Portuguese: a) What is the *micro-conto* about? Analyse the text, identifying its three layers: theme, events that precede those described, and characters. b) Imagine an alternative ending to the *micro-conto*(s). c) Explain why you chose the *micro-conto*(s) and its/their relevance to contemporary culture. d) If you opted for two texts, you an discuss their similarities and differences.

A key feature of *micro-contos* is that they hint at a lot of information which is left out of the text. This means that the reader has to construct meaning from very few elements and it is crucial to consider every detail to decode the message.

Micro-contos are also usually ambiguous and the reader must make decisions based on subtle linguistic elements to infer meaning or justify an interpretation. I introduced a selected *micro-conto* to the class who explored relevant linguistic elements, or "salient features" (Tomlinson, 2011, p. 7), through close-reading. Take the example below:

> "Aqueles dois olhos luminosos, destacados na noite, avançavam em sua direção. Quando o alcançaram, uma buzina foi a última coisa que ouviu" (Seabra, n.d.).

In this *micro-conto*, 'dois olhos luminosos' could refer to the bright eyes of a person or animal, but the association with the word 'buzina' (horn) in the second sentence suggests a metaphor for the headlights of a car/truck/van. We know however that the vehicle is not a motorbike because there are two headlights. Similarly, from the first sentence we can infer that one thing is heading in the direction of something else, but we do not yet know the gender of these objects/ beings. However, the use of the masculine singular pronoun 'o' in the second sentence – 'Quando o alcançaram' – indicates that it is a male/masculine person/ animal/object. These cryptic lines encapsulate a story that the learners must try to articulate. The *conto* is meant to spur learners' creativity and imagination within the constraints of the text and learners have to explain what, in their opinion, the text is describing. There are many possibilities but these are not limitless.

I then introduced the iceberg theory (Collie & Slater, 1987), a writing method used to suggest underlying themes without explicitly mentioning them, according to which the text of the *micro-conto* is the visible tip of the iceberg and below the surface are the other elements, i.e. the sequence of events until the moment captured by the text; the characters and their story; and the theme or wider context (see Figure 2).

Figure 2. The iceberg theory[3]

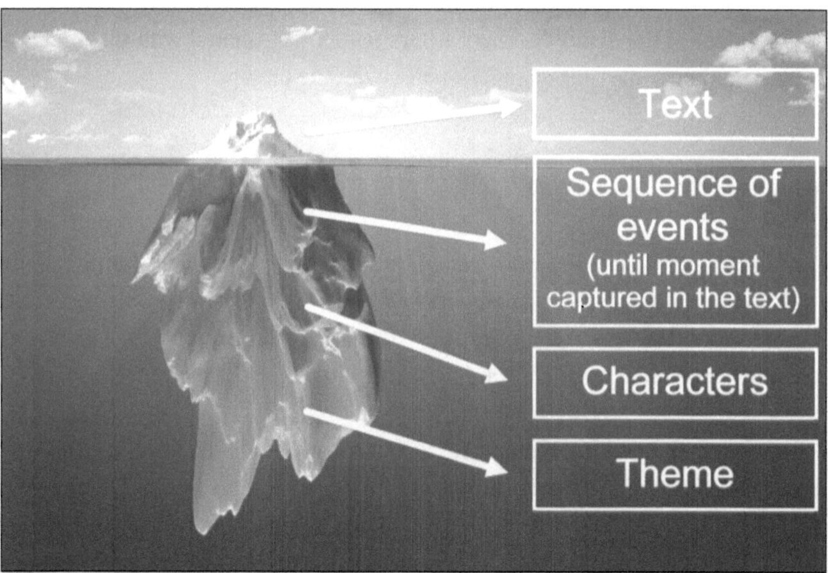

After students collectively identified how these layers related to the initial text, the class was split into small groups and each chose one *micro-conto* from a sample of five, on which they repeated the iceberg analysis and close-reading, before sharing their thoughts with the whole class. Admittedly, a mixture of L1 and L2 was used throughout, with more confident students attempting answers in L2. I gave positive reinforcement to these attempts but I also recognise that this is a challenging activity and that if learners attempted an explanation of the text in L1 they were still engaging positively with the input in the target language. I gave feedback to groups, while guiding their reading strategies before thoughts were shared by the groups. Some groups picked the same text which led to a fruitful discussion and students pointed out what was challenging in their text by clarifying new idioms, vocabulary, and difficult grammar points for the benefit of the whole class.

---

3. Illustration adapted from César Henrique de Santis Nascimento's image (Public domain); https://www.flickr.com/photos/146896964@N02/28928783864

In the following class, learners used the iceberg structure to write a *micro-conto* in groups. I offered images as prompts, but not everyone took them. Each group had to identify the distinct iceberg layers which they shared with the tutor, but they shared only the finished *micro-conto* with the class.

4.   Discussion

The ambiguous nature of *micro-contos* allows for several possible interpretations, which challenged learners and enabled them to practise problem-solving. Furthermore, by writing a *micro-conto,* learners could exercise their creativity and further develop an understanding and appreciation for the genre.

This approach to skills development through creativity goes hand in hand with positive affect. On the latter, Tomlinson (2011, p. 7) suggests that learners who achieve positive affect are more motivated and are much more likely to achieve communicative competence. Occasionally, I observed that a student did not respond enthusiastically to the text read in class. To counter this, I allowed for freedom of text choice, i.e. a choice of five texts for the in-class group activity, and a list of online sources to choose from for the assessed piece). This not only allowed for further exposure to the target language but also required self-investment and facilitated a learner-centred discovery which, once more, is suggested by Tomlinson as good practice (Tomlinson, 2011, p. 12), and led to lowering affective barriers. Furthermore, the range of activities – reading, analysing, writing, discussing – cater for different learning styles while encouraging intellectual and emotional involvement which can lead to a deeper and more durable learning (Tomlinson, 2011, pp. 18, 21-22).

Finally, Tomlinson (2011) proposes that feedback should have a focus on communicative effectiveness rather than on accuracy. In this case study, the individually-written assessed coursework was the culmination of the activity with formative feedback being an essential element. The tutor not only highlighted linguistic features that needed attention or that were well used, but also focused on the analysis and communicative effectiveness of the text so that learners could gauge which linguistic structures were most effective. Federici (2017) echoes Tomlinson (2011) in stressing the importance of valuing effective communication and offers a successful model for developing writing skills by presenting learners with a clear purpose and offering formative feedback along the planning stages with a focus on communication rather than sentence-level accuracy.

Overall, the individual pieces of coursework not only were a meaningful analysis but signalled a clear departure from the CEFR A2 communication "in areas of immediate need" in the direction of producing B1 "connected text on topics which are [...] of personal interest" (CEFR, n.d., p. 24). And, even though there was no formal mechanism for capturing feedback on this activity specifically, the returns in the general module questionnaires that were distributed at the end of the semester were very revealing. Nearly seven weeks after the activity was conducted in class, it was still mentioned by several students as their favourite part of the module which confirms the impact of this learning activity on fostering positive affect. Other points praised by learners were the exposure to authentic materials, the enjoyable analysis methodology, and the usefulness of the approach. Another positive result of this activity was that students really enjoyed reading literary texts and, although this goes beyond the remit of this paper, it would be interesting to enquire how far the use of *micro-contos* has contributed to changing learners' attitudes towards these types of texts.

5.   Conclusion

In this paper I have demonstrated that adopting Tomlinson's (2011) principles to develop materials using *micro-contos* has enhanced the learning experience and helped learners progress from CEFR A2 to B1 in Portuguese. By presenting them with clear and stimulating communicative purposes, allied to engaging input and opportunities for formative feedback, I have facilitated the development of learners' language skills as well as transferable soft skills, such as analytical, creative, and problem-solving skills.

References

Almeida, A. B., & Puig, I. (2017). Enhancing employability skills by bringing literature back in the foreign language class. In C. Álvarez-Mayo, A. Gallagher-Brett & F. Michel (Eds), *Innovative language teaching and learning at university: enhancing employability* (pp. 105-112). Research-publishing.net. https://doi.org/10.14705/rpnet.2017.innoconf2016.660

Born Global. (2016). *Born global: implications for higher education*. The British Academy. https://www.thebritishacademy.ac.uk/publications/born-global-implications-higher-education/

CEFR. (n.d.). *Common European framework of reference for languages: learning, teaching, assessment*. European year of languages 2001. https://rm.coe.int/1680459f97

Collie, J., & Slater, S. (1987). *Literature in the language classroom*. Cambridge University Press.

Federici, T. (2017). Enhancing students' potential: EBL projects in language teaching. In C. Álvarez-Mayo, A. Gallagher-Brett & F. Michel (Eds), *Innovative language teaching and learning at university: enhancing employability* (pp. 89-95). Research-publishing.net. https://doi.org/10.14705/rpnet.2017.innoconf2016.658

Seabra, C. (n.d.). *Microcontos*. http://www.seabra.com/contos/index1.html

Tomlinson, B. (2011). Introduction: principles and procedures of materials development. In B. Tomlinson (Ed.), *Materials development in language teaching* (pp. 1-31). Cambridge University Press.

7 'La ballata dell'amore cieco': a case study on the use of songs in Italian language learning

Salvatore Campisi[1]

Abstract

The song 'La ballata dell'amore cieco (o della vanità)' (1966), by Italian singer-songwriter Fabrizio De André (1940-1999), offers students opportunities to practise their language skills, stimulate their cultural appreciation, and expand their knowledge of a musical and poetic form (the ballad), while reflecting on the close connection between poetry and dance. Moving from receptive to productive skills, from gist to detail, learning activities are staged over three sessions, where students examine the song's musical features and lyrics and then produce their own ballads in writing. The paper first discusses the benefits and pitfalls of using songs as a tool to develop linguistic skills and raise cultural awareness. It then describes the learning opportunities offered by De André's song and concludes with an evaluation of the effectiveness of these activities, examining the potential for further research.

Keywords: student engagement, language and culture, music and language learning, poetry and dance.

---

1.   Introduction

Despite activating different brain functions and neural pathways, music and language are intimately connected. In evolutionary terms, speech has

---

1. The University of Manchester, Manchester, United Kingdom; salvatore.campisi@manchester.ac.uk; https://orcid.org/0000-0002-5072-2891

How to cite this chapter: Campisi, S. (2020). 'La ballata dell'amore cieco': a case study on the use of songs in Italian language learning. In A. B. Almeida, U. Bavendiek & R. Biasini (Eds), *Literature in language learning: new approaches* (pp. 59-67). Research-publishing.net. https://doi.org/10.14705/rpnet.2020.43.1096

---

emerged from human development and the use of sounds (Khaghaninejad & Fahandejsaadi, 2016, p. 90). Babies, who are not able to distinguish between singing and speaking, learn the 'music' of a language before using it communicatively (Stansell, 2005, pp. 6-8). Music and language share features such as pitch, intonation, and stress. There is, therefore, a good degree of overlapping and mutual cognitive support between abilities that pertain to music and language.

From the literature surveyed, music and/or songs can make a positive impact on language acquisition in broadly three areas: motivation, linguistic development, and cultural competency.

Engaging students with activities based on songs certainly adds variety to teaching and learning and "represents a change of pace in the classroom" (Chandler, 2016, p. 25), but it does not necessarily translate into increased motivation, as scholars sometimes too hastily indicate (e.g. Stansell, 2005). There are at least four variables that determine student engagement in this context: students' interests in music; whether they relate to the genre or the song they have been asked to work on; their preferred learning style; and the teacher's approach and personality, as aptly suggested by Fisher (2001, p. 47).

Selecting a song that sparks curiosity in the learners can indeed be challenging. From my own experience with learners of Italian in a British university context, students are not generally drawn to Italian (vocal) music. Although a small number are opera enthusiasts, the majority finds the genre dated, nor are students excited about overly sentimental Italian pop music, or Italian rap, which they often perceive as less appealing than its Anglophone models.

Linguistically, a song can be exploited to focus on pronunciation, as well as to consolidate and expand vocabulary and grammar. Songs can help students familiarise themselves with pronunciation and boost their confidence when reusing a given word or phrase; however, the prosody of a language changes when it is sung (see Leith, 1979), and many songs include words pronounced with an unnatural stress in order to accommodate a given rhyming pattern or for other intended effects (see Chandler, 2016). Furthermore, songs in a regional dialect can be productive for advanced levels but potentially misleading and confusing for beginners and intermediate students.

Songs have intrinsic qualities that can be fruitfully exploited for vocabulary acquisition and grammar development, "since many people often remember rhyme, rhythm or melody better than ordinary speech" (Failoni, 1993, p. 98), but the combined effect and interplay of music and text can be 'distracting' for the learner: "when the music was too difficult or the melody remained unlearned, it had the opposite effect on recall" (Khaghaninejad & Fahandejsaadi, 2016, p. 26).

Moreover, compared to more traditional drills and language tasks, songs offer students exposure to 'authentic language', often rich in colloquialisms and slang, and can be a valuable mnemonic device to internalise a given grammar rule, without the need to recall a formal definition (see Chandler, 2016, pp. 23-25). However, exposure to ungrammatical structures, very common in song lyrics, combined with the fact that songs can stick in our minds, can interfere with the learner's acquisition of grammar at lower levels: the use of a double negative in *(I can't get no) Satisfaction* by The Rolling Stones is a case in point.

Songs can also enhance cultural competency and appreciation, given that lyrics (e.g. references to social and political issues) and/or music (melody, rhythm, and instrumentation) may contain elements which are representative of the target culture(s). It is therefore advisable to avoid songs which replicate a foreign model or genre too closely without affording insights into the target culture(s), or songs that may perpetuate stereotypes and clichés about the target culture(s), as Griffin (1977, p. 943) notes in relation to the reception of Hispanic musical culture in the United States.

2.   Methodology

This case study includes a sequence of learning activities based on *La ballata dell'amore cieco (o della vanità)* (1966), a song written by Italian singer-songwriter Fabrizio De André (1940-1999). Both the music and the lyrics include elements which would be difficult to categorise as typically Italian. The learning activities rely on this element of novelty to spark students' curiosity and trigger their reflection on their perception of Italian music. Students also learn more about a musical and poetic form (the ballad) as well as the relation between poetry and dance.

The lyrics, appropriate for advanced learners, offer students an opportunity to revise certain elements of grammar and acquire new vocabulary. Moving from gist to detail, and from receptive to productive skills, tasks are spread over three sessions.

In the first stage, students are presented with six questions in Italian before the first playback: What do you think about the song? What emotions does it evoke? What images does it conjure up? What are the lyrics about? Do you listen to Italian music? Is this song a representative example of Italian music?

Students are then asked to listen to the song and focus on the first four questions, which aim to canvass their personal reactions and understanding of the song and lyrics. After the first playback, students discuss their answers in pairs, or small groups, before opening the discussion to the whole class. The role of the tutor is to facilitate the discussion during this phase. Students learn more on the song through a gap-fill exercise on the lyrics, which also helps them revise articles, pronouns, and possessive adjectives (see sample stanza in Figure 1).

Figure 1. Gap-fill exercise

> **NUOVO ASCOLTO E RICOSTRUZIONE DEL TESTO**
> articoli, pronomi e aggettivi possessivi in evidenza
>
> ... uomo onesto, ... uomo ......,
> tralalalalla tralallaleru
> ... innamorò ....
> ... ... che non ... amava niente.

At this point, after playing the song a second time and checking their answers in the gap-fill exercise, pairs or small groups are asked to consider the lyrics in relation to the music (melody, rhythm, instrumentation) and answer the remaining two questions they were presented at the beginning.

After helping students examine the lyrics in more detail and clarifying any unknown vocabulary, the tutor elicits comments on both the lyrics and the structure of the song (e.g. division verse/chorus, rhyming patterns). Students' attention is finally drawn to the word 'ballata' in the title. For the following session, they are invited to research the ballad form in both musical and poetic terms and then think of other examples of ballads they may be familiar with.

At the beginning of the second session, students discuss their findings and provide examples of ballads. During the discussion, they are invited to reflect on the intimate connection between music and poetry and are finally asked to compose their own ballads following a given rhyming scheme which, as in all ballads, includes a refrain (see line marked with 'x' in Figure 2).

Figure 2. Ballad scheme

SCRIVIAMO LE NOSTRE BALLATE

Un giorno al mARE (x)

Era un'estate torrida ed afOSA (a)
ed io me ne stavo distESO, (b)
mi si avvicinò una persona famOSA (a)
che mi disse di sloggiARE (x)

io che ero ancora assopITO (c)
le dissi di andare a quel paESE, (d)
tanto ne fui indispettITO; (c)
la stupida si mise allora a gridARE (x)

coprendomi d'insulti e parolACCE (e)
dandomi del troglodITA (f)
mi disse ch'ero buono a vendere focACCE (e)
furibondo e sbalordito, io la volevo schiaffeggiARE (x)

Students are divided into groups of six to eight students and each group has to compose their own ballad on the institution's virtual learning environment (Blackboard) before the final session. Each student is expected to contribute one to two lines, depending on the group size, and their line(s) should not only follow the rhyming scheme but also coherently fit with the lines previously written by peers. Ballads are shown and discussed in class in the final session and have occasionally been included in the departmental newsletter (see Figure 3).

Figure 3. Students' ballads

SE SOLO SAPESSI CHE TI SONO ACCANTO	PENSIERI DI UN PASTORE TEDESCO	IL MIO PROMBLEMINO CON IL CUCCHIANO
Dammi qualche minuto Ti dirò tutto ciò che tu vorrai mai sapere, Il futuro che ho immaginato fatto di noi e della nostra vita insieme. Mentre il viaggio sarebbe lungo Il nostro amore sarà forte e profondo Al tuo fianco mi pongo Non ti nascondere da me. Dammi la tua mano di nuovo E asciuga bene le lacrime Tutte queste sensazioni meravigliose dal mio cuore provengono Sembra come un amore programmato per noi due. (Clare, Andrew, Franky, Suzanne, Floriana, Petrit, Meritxell)	Il giorno era lungo e freddoloso, così mi sentivo come un pazzo fuori di me, come un pazzo arrabbiato e geloso Provavo ancora qualcosa per te. E così gironzolavo per le strade, Non potevo pensare ad un'altra, Sei veramente la luce delle mie lampade, Oh perché non provi a brillare per me! Il giorno è venuto, ho voluto sapere Quanto ancora mi vuoi o se è tutto finito, Risolvo i problemi cominciando a bere, È l'unica cosa che faccio per te. (Owen, Naomi, Martin, Fay, Daisy, Jennifer, Ed, Will)	Era un giorno scuro e piovoso, seguii alcuni passi al carnevale, Ma, una cosa molto fastidiosa, Non potevo trovare il mio favorito cucchiaino! Il giorno dopo era soleggiato, così, ho camminato sulla spiaggia, poi ad un bar, prendo un caffé macchiato, Dove ho chiacchierato con un uomo di Torino. Dopo un'ora mi sembrava una cosa, Quest'uomo era infatti una donna, Era proprio strana questa settimana, perché la cosa più curiosa... Era che lei teneva il mio cucchiaino! (By Ian, Tom, Hannah, James, Caroline, Sarah, Julie, Rebecca)

3.   Findings

I designed the learning activities above in the academic year 2009-2010 and have developed and adapted them since. They have generally received a very positive response from students and elicited their interest and curiosity. However, the overall engagement and enthusiasm has varied, also depending on students' interest in music and Italian music in particular.

Engagement with the group composition of a ballad (formative writing task) has also varied considerably. Students more naturally inclined to a divergent (imaginative) mode of thinking took the task as an opportunity to practise their language skills creatively, and this emerged from the attention they put in framing their lines and their word choices, whereas students more drawn to convergent (factual) thinking may have felt that the task was not particularly appealing to their learning style or that there was limited scope for writing practice in composing a couple of lines for a ballad (Marashi & Tahan-Shizari, 2015).

The themes, tone, and quality of the ballads were also heterogeneous, and ranged from generically romantic (see the first two columns in Figure 3) to humorous/nonsensical (final column). Irrespective of students' appreciation of the song or overall engagement, the learning activities have had two important merits, which I felt most students valued in light of their comments during and at the end of the activities. Firstly, the tasks drew students' attention to Italian music, a cultural aspect that is generally peripheral in academic curricula, and challenged their idea or perception of Italian modern popular music. The song was different from stereotypical ideas of Italian music, it was not an aria, nor could it be classed as mainstream pop music. The song chorus recalls the sound of a jazz big band, De André's singing style is close to French chansonniers and Leonard Cohen, and the upbeat jazzy rhythm contrasts with the sombre lyrics, which tell the gruesome story of a twisted love affair (find song with lyrics in A Study in Floyd, 2011).

The second important merit is that these learning activities have led students to research and reflect on an important poetic and musical form, the ballad, and the close connection between poetry and dance, which are often thought of as diametrically opposite forms of art: the former, mental and (extremely) serious, and the latter, physical and often associated with (light) entertainment.

4.   Conclusion

Although choosing a suitable song for the relevant learning stage can be challenging, an appropriate song is a versatile resource that allows students to practise all language skills (listening, speaking, reading, and writing) and grammar. It can also increase their cultural awareness and engage them beyond the immediate language or culture-specific context. A syllabus that includes activities based on music and/or songs is more varied and inclusive, as it caters for those students who are auditory learners or have a predominant musical-rhythmic intelligence.

Both my perspective and findings have limitations that future iterations of the learning activities and further research can address. It would therefore be interesting to widen the perspective by exploring the response of learners from a different cultural background or in a different learning context, or the engagement of students of other languages in similar learning activities. Future administration of pre- and post-intervention questionnaires could also assess the effectiveness of the learning activities in terms of cultural awareness development (i.e. whether tasks have helped students reformulate their perspective on Italian music) and further substantiate my observations and findings.

References

A Study in Floyd. (2011, April 22). *Ballata dell'Amore cieco o della Vanità (testo) - Fabrizio de André* [Video file]. https://youtu.be/6t5KRvu7xRY

Chandler, C. M. (2016). *The relationship between music and language: can teaching with songs result in improved second language learning?* Graduation thesis. Texas State University. https://digital.library.txstate.edu/handle/10877/6081

Failoni, J. W. (1993). Music as means to enhance cultural awareness and literacy in the foreign language classroom. *Mid-Atlantic Journal of Foreign Language Pedagogy, 1*(Spr), 97-108.

Fisher, D. (2001). Early language learning with and without music. *Reading Horizons, 42*(1), 39-49. https://scholarworks.wmich.edu/reading_horizons/vol42/iss1/3

Griffin, R. J. (1977). Teaching Hispanic culture through folk music. *Hispania, 60*(4), 942-45. https://doi.org/10.2307/340674

Khaghaninejad, M. S., & Fahandejsaadi, R. (2016). *Music and language learning.* Katibe-Novin.

Leith, W. D. (1979). Advanced French conversation through popular music. *The French Review 52*(4), 537-551.

Marashi H., & Tahan-Shizari, P. (2015). Using convergent and divergent tasks to improve writing and language learning motivation. *Iranian Journal of Language Teaching Research, 3*(1), 99-117.

Stansell, J. W. (2005). *The use of music for learning languages: a review of the literature.* University of Illinois at Urbana-Champaign. http://writingthetrueself.com/pdfs/Jon_Stansell_The_Use_of_Music_for_Learning_Languages.pdf

8 When the reader becomes the writer; creative writing approaches in the foreign language classroom

Anke Bohm[1] and Hanna Magedera-Hofhansl[2]

Abstract

Using a contemporary short story by the award-winning German writer Roman Ehrlich as a case study, in this paper we will offer ideas for engaging students at CEFR (Common European Framework of Reference for languages) B1+ and B2 level in German in reading as well as encouraging them in creative writing tasks through formative assessment and coursework. More specifically, we will argue that literature in the classroom is a means of practising reading comprehension. This opens up opportunities for students to create their own literary texts, with receptive skills becoming productive skills. Introducing two projects we carried out with students in their first and second years at the University of Liverpool as examples, we will discuss process and practice. We will show how reading and writing projects can be linked to aspects of authentic assessment and its forms. We are then going to explore the possibilities for further embedding literary assessments in coursework, highlighting their benefits and challenges, including the process of publishing them on a student-led WordPress site.

Keywords: Roman Ehrlich, creative writing, interactive class participation, student engagement, authentic assessment.

---

1. University of Manchester, Manchester, United Kingdom; anke.bohm@manchester.ac.uk

2. University of Liverpool, Liverpool, United Kingdom; hofhansl@liverpool.ac.uk

How to cite this chapter: Bohm, A., & Magedera-Hofhansl, H. (2020). When the reader becomes the writer; creative writing approaches in the foreign language classroom. In A. B. Almeida, U. Bavendiek & R. Biasini (Eds), *Literature in language learning: new approaches* (pp. 69-75). Research-publishing.net. https://doi.org/10.14705/rpnet.2020.43.1097

---

1.   Introduction

In this paper we are going to explore how the stay of a writer in residence can be used as a platform to engage students in developing core language skills; in reading, analysing, listening, speaking, interpreting, mastering advanced grammar and, just as importantly, writing. We will also explore how to make use of residencies, so they continue to have an impact *after* an author's visit.

Reading and translating literary texts stand among the oldest approaches to learning languages. Across millennia, initiates have had to read exemplary texts and translate them from, *inter alia*, Hebrew, Greek, Latin, etc. into their own tongue. Considered old-fashioned by the mid-twentieth century, contemporary pedagogies have emphasised production rather than reception within a communicative rather than textual paradigm. In recent years, we are witnessing a return to literary texts as attractive and authentic additions to communicative pedagogies at our institutions, see e.g. Di Martino and Di Sabato (2014).

2.   Uses of literature in class: translation, poetry, novels

Against the background described in the introduction, we have sought to experiment with literary texts at the University of Liverpool in ways that promote student engagement. For example, we introduce students at B1 and B2 levels to excerpts drawn from German literary texts which are both informative and humorous, such as Koppensteiner's (1984) *Österreich erzählt*. Alongside newspaper stories covering current affairs which inform students about political and social issues and introduce them to higher level reading comprehension skills, we also give them extracts from novels from several German-speaking countries. Our aim is to choose texts that encourage our students to read the full book for their oral exams which, in German at Liverpool, are the basis of their assessments in Years 1 and 2 at levels B1 and B2.

However, our pedagogical practice with literature in language learning has gone beyond the above. As part of moving from reception to production and the development of creative writing tasks, we want to emphasise the attractiveness of short stories in particular. Short stories as a genre are easily manageable for most levels of language learner while remaining rewarding to read. Students are also offered choice with an option of short stories from a pool, allowing them to follow their interests. It was in experimenting with short stories in particular that we saw the possibilities offered by a literary residency for extending our teaching and learning practices. In what follows we will describe how we organised the residency before drawing out more general lessons from that experience of relevance to those interested in using literature in the language classroom.

3. Literature-based classroom activities and assessment

In February 2018, the contemporary German author Roman Ehrlich, born in 1983 in Aichach, Bavaria, began a residency at the University of Liverpool and Lancaster University. Financed partly by the Writer in Residence (WiR) programme of the DAAD (German Academic Exchange Service) and partly by internal university funds as part of a collaboration, Ehrlich stayed in Liverpool for a week and interactively participated in a number of different language and content seminars across all year groups within the German degree programme.

Before the visit, we began to use *Das Gesuch (An Appeal)*[3], a 12 page-long short story from Ehrlich's (2014) collection *Urwaldgäste* as the basis for formative and summative assessments as well as classroom activities with students in their first (post A-Level) and second year of studies. Within the story, various storylines chart characters living through various situations which together form a pool of possibilities to capture the students' attention and allow them to engage with the story from multiple perspectives. Those situations included, *inter alia,*

---

3. We have used the acknowledged but as of yet unpublished translation of 'Das Gesuch' 'An Appeal' by Elke Wardlaw.

a person trying to convince their supervisor to be allowed to change jobs, a former teacher participating in a quiz show, and an IT-engineer borrowing a pornography DVD in a video store. Narratives of this kind are especially suited for classroom work due to the large number of places where readers can fill in gaps in the storyline according to their own understanding. Filling in those gaps allows students to use their imagination while working within the narrative and linguistic scaffold provided by the author.

In addition to introducing this literary material, a number of other steps were taken to prepare the students for the author's visit. Over the Christmas break, the students of Year 1 (B1) read the entire short story and, upon their return, worked in class in groups of four to develop a deeper textual understanding as well as to identify the different primary plotlines within the story. The five main plotlines featured in Ehrlich's (2014) short story were formally separated rather than interwoven. Following that, every student chose a character they were intrigued by and new groups were formed based on their decisions in order to carry out a language analysis of the character's own story, a means, which, according to Hall (2016), supports the language learning process. As the storylines were neither action-laden nor fast-paced and the characters often focused on being in the moment, the tutor chose to practise a more mindful approach to gain a deeper appreciation of the text. The results of the analyses were presented by the students to the rest of the seminar-group.

In the course of Ehrlich's visit, the students' analyses were complemented by a meet-the-author Q&A session where the students were given the opportunity to ask questions based on their analyses. The following year we ran the same project again. While the author was not present, the students were still encouraged to think about the questions they would ask him and then to come up with likely answers for themselves.

Based on all the information collected, students then chose a character they wanted to focus on for a 500-word assignment. For this written assessment, the students had to write either a prequel or sequel to their favourite character's storyline in a first-person perspective. The students were encouraged to write creatively; however, they were also reassured that less creativity would not lead to a lower mark, as a creative element can sometimes cause worry in this regard. The mark for the assignment was based predominantly on the command of language they demonstrated in terms of range, accuracy, and style, as well as coherence.

For the second year cohort (B2), a very specific gap in the storyline of one of the characters was picked for the students to fill: a woman participating in a TV quiz show asked during her appearance why she no longer wanted to be a teacher. In her answer to this question she refers to a dream she has had, but she does not give any further information, either to the audience in the text or to the reader. The formative assessment based on the teacher "Frau S. aus P.'s" tale asked students to write 150-200 words narrating the dream's content.

Students responded to both tasks very creatively and they led to a generally high level of engagement with Ehrlich's story as a piece of contemporary German literature. The coursework produced during these experiments with literature was also of a high standard and was enjoyed by participating students as highlighted in the end in the module evaluation questionnaires. Our experiences suggest, therefore, that literary residencies can be highly effective indeed.

4.   Lessons drawn: didactics of a literary residency

Based on our experiences, we suggest the following steps to make best use of a literary residency.

First, work by visiting authors should be introduced *before* they arrive via texts whose length can be adjusted according to learning level as part of reading comprehension. This involves different reading tasks: global comprehension, i.e. overall structure and meaning; analysis of language use and style; unusual vocabulary/use of words from specific regions; punctuation; longer or shorter sentences vis-à-vis rhythm and speed; and choice of genre. Translating a text requires comprehension of exact detail as well as its cultural and country-specific features. Given this, translation and its challenges prepare the students for an author's visit.

Second, once students have a thorough grasp of the text, they should prepare questions to discuss in person with the author *during* their residency. Discussion topics can cover biographical questions as a lead up to more textually oriented questions about the work and its production and meaning. Students can demonstrate specific knowledge of the texts by asking detailed questions about certain characters their classroom work has focused on. To avoid silence when the author actually visits, these questions should be well-prepared and ready to hand. Meet-the-author Q&A sessions constitute authentic speaking and listening situations involving engagement with the author's answers in real-time which incorporates a contextualised perspective of real readers (see Swann & Allington, 2009).

Finally, *post-residency*, students can be asked to write blogs about the author's visit in English for their university, interview fellow students on what they liked best about the texts and the experience of meeting the author, and engage further with the author's texts by writing online reviews on public or internal university platforms. At the University of Liverpool, final year students in German created a WordPress site called *Der Hammer* which allowed for wider impact and accessibility.

5.   Conclusion

There are many ways of using literature in the classroom, such as translating extracts from novels, reading poetry aloud, and reading novels for an oral exam. We have mentioned only a few options here, concentrating on literary residencies in particular. As we have shown, literary residencies, as authentic teaching and learning situations, stimulate more engagement with the subject in general over several weeks from the preparation of the visit, to live Q&As, to the post-preparation of writing a blog and assessed coursework in final exams. We cannot, therefore, recommend them highly enough. Admittedly, an author's visit is a special occasion, but with modern technology, visits can be virtual as well as physical through live chats or video calls. The projects can be expanded by liaison interpreting – live or via video-call – to subtitling an existing video about an author or by creating a short film about an author and his or her work. The options are endless, and we would encourage those involved in language teaching to explore them for themselves.

References

Di Martino, E., & Di Sabato, B. (2014). *Studying language through literature: an old perspective revisited and something more*. Cambridge Scholars Publishing.

Ehrlich, R. (2014). Das Gesuch. In R. Ehrlich, *Urwaldgäste, Erzählungen* (pp. 157-172). Dumont.

Hall, G. (2016). Stylistics in second language contexts: a critical perspective. In G. Watson & S. Zyngier (Eds), *Literature and stylistics for language learners, theory and practice* (pp. 3-14). Palgrave Macmillan. https://doi.org/10.1057/9780230624856_1

Koppensteiner, J. (1984). (Ed.). *Österreich erzählt, ein Lesebuch für Deutschlernende*. Bundesverlag ÖBV.

Swann, J., & Allington, D. (2009). Reading groups and the language of literary texts: a case study in social reading. *Language and Literature, 18*(3), 247-264. https://doi.org/10.1177/0963947009105852

9 French creative theatre in a course for beginners: the case of 'Finissez vos phrases!' by Jean Tardieu

Géraldine Crahay[1]

Abstract

This article discusses the benefits of theatrical texts in language courses for beginners. These original, fun, and yet challenging materials help learners develop linguistic and intercultural competencies and transferable skills such as critical thinking, problem-solving, and cooperation. Specifically, this article examines the use of Jean Tardieu's (2000/1955) short comedy *Finissez vos phrases!* in a French course for beginners at university level. The particularities of this play are its brevity and the incompleteness of its dialogues. I argue that studying Tardieu's (2000/1955) comedy allows learners to develop their communication skills by reading the whole play, watching a performance of the play, completing the dialogues, and performing their new version in front of the class. Moreover, *Finissez vos phrases!* familiarises learners with French conversational conventions and encourages them to think about the effectiveness of language. It also enhances their cooperative skills, lets them express their creativity and, ultimately, offers them a playful approach to learning French.

Keywords: literature and language, theatre, creative writing, conversational conventions, Jean Tardieu, beginners.

1. Durham University, Durham, United Kingdom; geraldine.crahay@durham.ac.uk

How to cite this chapter: Crahay, G. (2020). French creative theatre in a course for beginners: the case of 'Finissez vos phrases!' by Jean Tardieu. In A. B. Almeida, U. Bavendiek & R. Biasini (Eds), *Literature in language learning: new approaches* (pp. 77-84). Research-publishing.net. https://doi.org/10.14705/rpnet.2020.43.1098

1.   Introduction

The language of literary texts is often considered to be different from ordinary language (Hall, 2005, pp. 9-38; Kramsch, 1993, p. 130) and, for this reason, too difficult at the lower levels of language learning. Except for Lazar (1993), most scholars examining the use of literature in language teaching run quickly through the case of beginners or ignore it altogether to focus on more advanced levels.

The Council of Europe's Common European Framework of Reference for Languages, or CEFR, corroborates this view. The first version of the descriptors of the different levels only referred to the use of literary texts from B2 level on: "I can understand contemporary literary prose" (Council of Europe, 2001, p. 6). The new descriptors, published in 2018, are more detailed (Council of Europe, 2018, p. 65). They extend their use to A2 and B1 levels, as well as clarifying the literary genres (comics, songs, poems, short stories, novels, and non-fiction texts). However, they still omit the A1 level, prefer simple non-literary texts, and do not refer to theatre.

In this article, I make the claim that literary texts are not too difficult for language courses for beginners because, as Hall (2005) points out, they are "linguistically less distinctive and unrepresentative of the wider language than has traditionally been claimed" (p. 2). On the contrary, literary texts, and notably theatrical texts, should be introduced in the language classroom as soon as possible because they can help learners develop linguistic and intercultural competences. Moreover, they enhance creativity, an essential part of communicative competence (Hall, 2005, p. 28) that characterises literary and everyday languages (Atkins & Carter, 2012; Hall, 2005, p. 27).

To illustrate the relevance of theatrical texts in the language classroom, I discuss the case of the short play *Finissez vos phrases!* by the French author Jean Tardieu (2000/1955) in a French *ab initio* elective (but credit-bearing) module taught at Durham University during the academic year 2018/2019.

2.   Jean Tardieu and *Finissez vos phrases!*

The French playwright Jean Tardieu (1903-1995) wrote short comedies that played with words and invited the readers and audience to think about the meaning of words and the conventional aspect of communication. Conversations are so submitted to norms that the words that they use are often irrelevant in conveying meaning.

The play *Finissez vos phrases!* is both playful and challenging because, as the title teasingly suggests, all the sentences in the dialogues are unfinished. As the example below shows, keywords are missing. Yet, this oddity does not impede the overall understanding of the play. For instance, in the following interaction, the reader can understand that the two protagonists know and are greeting each other.

> "*Monsieur A, avec chaleur:* Chère amie. Quelle chance de vous…
> *Madame B, ravie:* Très heureuse, moi aussi. Très heureuse de… vraiment oui!
> *Monsieur A:* Comment allez-vous, depuis que?" (Tardieu, 2000/1955, p. 27).

Moreover, this comedy is suitable for beginners owing to its brevity (around 1,300 words), which means that the whole text can be read in class. *Finissez vos phrases!* is also characterised by the relative simplicity of its language and content. The play tells the story of two acquaintances, Monsieur A and Madame B, who meet in the street and start a conversation that they pursue in a café. The comedy accordingly appears genuine due to the universal banality of its synopsis and its language, which mirrors the hesitations of 'real' interactions.

3.   Organisation of the lessons

The lessons took place in the second term of the academic year 2018/2019 over six weeks. Between ten and thirty minutes were dedicated to *Finissez vos phrases!* each week, so that learners were not rushed into reading the play. The outcomes of the activities were to enhance communication skills (reading, listening, writing, and speaking), build vocabulary, revise grammar, and develop intercultural awareness and creativity.

The first activity consisted in reading a text about Jean Tardieu (2000/1955), adapted from the *Afterword* of the collection of his short plays. Students reflected upon the goals of Tardieu's (2000/1955) writing, listed the characteristics of a theatrical text, and thought about their behaviour when meeting an acquaintance by chance. These tasks aimed at highlighting the form, the content, and the particularities of the text. Students also read the beginning of the play (about 200 words) and explained the text's oddities. Learners' answers to the different tasks were discussed during the lesson and the incompleteness of the dialogues was highlighted.

The next in-class activity was watching the beginning of the play (which they already knew) performed by the *École de théâtre de Paris* (Paris Theatre School) in 2010[2]. Watching a performance of the play enabled students to hear the written words out loud and to appreciate how they were interpreted by French drama students. Learners also gathered implicit information that they may have missed when reading the text. For instance, most students found Monsieur A shy and strange and suggested that he was in love with Madame B. The actor's nervous gestures and his avoiding Madame B's eyes made this important storyline explicit. The activity highlighted the fact that non-verbal expression contributes to the meaning of a text.

Afterwards, the class was divided into groups of two or three students and each group received an extract of the play. Their task consisted in completing the dialogue of their extract. This transformational writing activity enabled learners to demonstrate their understanding of the play in a more progressive way than merely answering questions (see Hall, 2005, p. 150). As Pope (1995) pointed

---

2. http://www.dailymotion.com/video/xdso6a

out, "[t]he best way to understand how a text works [...] is to change it" (quoted by Parkinson & Reid Thomas, 2000, p. 38).

However, the purpose of the task went beyond mere reading comprehension. Firstly, students could think critically about sociolinguistic conventions. They realised that most everyday conversation can be understood even though it is truncated because it obeys implicit conversational rules (Clayman & Gill, 2012), for instance greeting an acquaintance and turn-taking.

Moreover, filling the gaps allowed students to revise French grammar and vocabulary, as they had to follow grammatical constraints when re-writing their extract. Importantly, the task helped them become aware that grammar actively contributes to the meaning of a text (Doniger, 2003, p. 101). For example, after declaring his love to Madame B, Monsieur A says: "Allons à! Allons au!" (Tardieu, 2000/1955, p. 35). Some students wrote: "Allons à LA MAISON! Allons au LIT!"[3], thus showing their understanding of contracted articles, i.e. the fact that the preposition *à* followed with the masculine singular definite article *le* becomes *au*, while it does not contract when followed with the feminine singular *la*.

Finally, the writing task valorised learners' creativity. Students enjoyed experimenting with the language and expressing familiar experiences (meeting an acquaintance, confessing one's love, etc.) with unfamiliar words (Kramsch, 1993, p. 171). A challenge was, however, comprehending that there were no right and wrong answers. The text of the play was a finished product that learners could transform as they liked. Grammar and idiomatic expressions conditioned some answers, but otherwise students had complete freedom. The best productions were often the most inventive ones. For instance, in one version, Madame B talks about her son, whose misfortune is marrying a wicked woman:

> "*Madame B (acceptant son bras, soudain volubile):* [...] Je pense encore à mon pauvre FILS. Il allait, comme ça, sans RIEN – ou plutôt

---

3. Words in capital letters are learners' additions (reproduced without modifications).

avec CETTE FILLE. Et tout à coup, voilà que ILS SONT MARIÉS! Ah là là! [...] Avoir eu tant de BONHEUR ET M'OUBLIER! Et voilà que plus IL RENTRE CHEZ LUI AVEC CETTE JEUNE FEMME DIABOLIQUE!" (after Tardieu, 2000/1955, p. 29).

Despite a few grammatical and stylistic blunders, Madame B's monologue is comprehensible, sophisticated, and entertaining.

After three writing sessions, learners performed their re-written extract in front of the class. Performing aimed at encouraging collaboration, improving spoken language (Parkinson & Reid Thomas, 2000, p. 123), and, above all, celebrating the text (Kramsch, 1993, p. 157). Some students brought props and costumes (wigs, berets, and drawings). Although the performance was formative, students still received informal feedback (see Table 1).

Table 1.   Feedback of the performance of the extract of *Finissez vos phrases!*

	ø	1	2	3	4	5	Comments
Content (originality)							
Language (grammar)							
Language (vocabulary)							
Speaking (pronunciation)							
Speaking (fluency)							
Performance (acting)							
Performance (props)							

4.   Conclusion

Some issues did arise during the classroom activities. One of them was the lack of clear indication of the gaps within Tardieu's (2000/1955) text. Creating the missing gaps could help students better understand the play, but, on the other hand, might restrict their creativity by imposing the teacher's interpretation of the text on them. Moreover, learners may lack the grammatical and lexical tools to deal with some difficulties, such as complex relative pronouns, the future tense, and the subjunctive mood.

Yet, despite these challenges, my conclusions are positive. I recommend using literature in the language classroom at elementary level. Theatrical texts constitute good learning resources owing to their dual nature: written and oral. They help learners develop communication skills, grammatical, lexical, and sociolinguistic competences, cooperation, creativity, and critical thinking. It is nevertheless necessary to prioritise simple texts (adapt them if needed) that are playful but still challenging in terms of content and/or reflections on language (about conversational rules, for instance). Deblase (2005), an English teacher who uses tableaux and soundscapes to teach literature, summarises the advantages of theatre in the classroom:

> "[u]sing drama to teach literature works because it invites students into the language of the text. [...] Students work collaboratively to interpret the text and its subtext. And because the students are responsible for revealing the meaning of the literary text, they become empowered rather than intimidated by language" (p. 32).

In reinterpreting the text, in appropriating its meaning through creative writing, learners become empowered by the text. Is empowering our students not our primary mission as teachers?

References

Atkins, S., & Carter, R. (2012). Creativity in speech. In J. P. Gee & M. Handford (Eds), *The Routledge handbook of discourse analysis* (pp. 315-325). Routledge.

Clayman, S. E., & Gill, V. T. (2012). Conversation analysis. In J. P. Gee & M. Handford (Eds), *The Routledge handbook of discourse analysis* (pp. 120-134). Routledge.

Council of Europe. (2001). *Common European framework of reference for languages: learning, teaching, assessment. Structured overview of All CEFR Scale.* https://rm.coe.int/168045b15e

Council of Europe. (2018). *Common European framework of reference for languages: learning, teaching, assessment. Companion volume with new descriptors.* https://rm.coe.int/cefr-companion-volume-with-new-descriptors-2018/1680787989

Deblase, G. (2005). Teaching literature and language through guided discovery and informal classroom drama. *The English Journal, 95*(1), 29-32. https://doi.org/10.2307/30047394

Doniger, P. E. (2003). Language matters: grammar as a tool in the teaching of literature. *The English Journal, 92*(3), 101-04. https://doi.org/10.2307/822268

Hall, G. (2005). *Literature in language education*. Palgrave Macmillan.

Kramsch, C. (1993). *Context and culture in language teaching*. Oxford University Press.

Lazar, G. (1993). *Literature and language teaching: a guide for teachers and trainers*. Cambridge University Press.

Parkinson, B., & Reid Thomas, H. (2000). *Teaching literature in a second language*. Edinburgh University Press.

Pope, R. (1995). *Textual interventions: critical and creative strategies for literary studies*. Routledge.

Tardieu, J. (2000/1955). *Finissez vos phrases!* Gallimard Jeunesse.

Author index